DIGITAL PHOTOGRAPHY

in easy steps

D0121203

NICK VANDOME

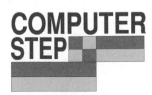

COMPUTER STEP

In easy steps is an imprint of Computer Step
Southfield Road . Southam
Warwickshire CV47 OFB . England

http://www.ineasysteps.com

Second edition

Notice of Liability

Every effort has been made to ensure that this book contains accurate and current information. However, Computer Step and the author shall not be liable for any loss or damage suffered by readers as a result of any information contained herein.

Trademarks

All trademarks are acknowledged as belonging to their respective companies.

Printed and bound in the United Kingdom

ISBN 1-84078-128-9

Table of Contents

4 Capturing digital images   63

5 Using Windows Me   85

6 Image editing software   93

The filmless camera

This chapter introduces the basics of digital photography and shows the uses to which it can be put. Web publishing, desktop publishing (DTP) and home use are discussed and there is a general introduction to the format and creation of digital images.

Covers

Chapter One

Defining digital photography

With recent advances in electronic and computing technology it seems like all of the familiar gadgets around us are being converted into digital versions: televisions, telephones, radios, camcorders and, of course, cameras. The main reasons for this are quality and speed of delivery of information.

Digital photography is a marriage between photographic techniques and computer technology. If you are interested in both then you will take to it like a duck to water. If your main interest is in one or other of the processes then you will have some enjoyable discoveries as you experience the other side of the equation.

Photography has been a willing participant in the digital revolution and it is now becoming established in both the commercial and consumer markets. At first sight, though, digital photography can appear confusing to the uninitiated: in addition to cameras there are computers, image editing software, printers, scanners and a host of other add-ons and peripherals. But the good news is that once some of the technical jargon has been stripped away digital photography is relatively straightforward: you take a picture in the traditional way but with a digital camera; you transfer the image onto a computer; you improve, enhance and edit the image; the final version is then printed, used on a Web page, or displayed on a monitor.

The starting point of any digital photography career is the camera. More and more of these are now appearing in both photographic and computer retail outlets and the choice and quality are increasing continually. Some digital cameras look almost identical to their film counterparts, so there is no need to readjust your perceptions on this front.

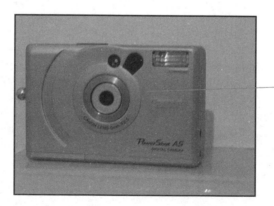

Digital cameras have a familiar look and feel to them

Using digital photography

There are a variety of ways of capturing digital images and using them but the basic process with a camera is:

In addition to capturing digital images with a camera, they can also be obtained with a scanner, a Photo CD, a video grabber or from the Internet.

1 Begin the digital process by capturing an image with a digital camera

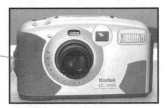

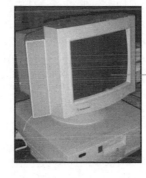

2 Edit the image on a computer

Digital images can also be viewed on a television or used in a multimedia presentation via a projector.

3 Print out a hard copy of the image

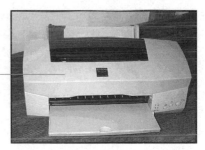

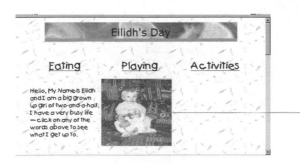

4 Use the image on a Web site

The first digital steps

The image sensors in the majority of digital cameras currently available are called Charge Coupled Devices (CCD). Another type, known as CMOS, is less widely used but gaining in popularity.

As far as capturing an image is concerned, digital photography differs very little from film photography. In both cases an image is seen through a viewing device and then light from the displayed image is recorded within the camera. It is in differing methods of recording the amount of light that the first big difference between film and digital photography lies. In the former, the light creates an image on photographic film. This is then developed into a photograph using a combination of chemicals. Digital photography is a lot less messy: the light that comes through the lens is recorded on a tiny computer chip (known as an image sensor). These contain hundreds of thousands or millions of devices called photosites, each of which stores electronic data about the amount of light that falls on it. Once the image has been captured by the image sensor this data is then sent to an Analogue to Digital Converter (ADC) which converts the image information into a format that can be interpreted by a computer.

An image sensor is a complex piece of equipment that is powered by some extremely fancy technology. The sensors currently available are equivalent to an ISO film rating of 100.

Once the photograph is taken, all similarity between traditional and digital photography ceases. A film image can be developed into a hard copy and that's pretty much it really. A digital image on the other hand can be transferred into a computer and, with the right software, numerous improvements can be made. Colours can be increased or decreased, unwanted objects can be removed (including spots, wrinkles and the dreaded red-eye), new items can be inserted and special effects can be applied.

Image editing programs range from programs costing £500 to free programs that can be downloaded from the Web.

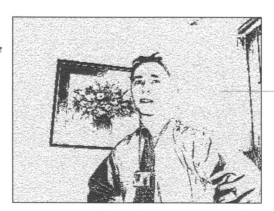

Effects such as this one are available in most image editing programs

The advantages of digital photography over its traditional counterpart are numerous and appealing:

- No more films to buy or process. A digital camera stores image on a reusable disc, or memory card, some of which can hold over 100 images before they are full:

Memory cards can be in the form of floppy discs, CompactFlash cards or SmartMedia cards. The type used will depend on the type of camera and each camera usually only uses one type of card.

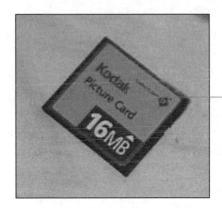

Memory cards are the digital answer to traditional film. They can hold a large amount of data and once you have downloaded your images you can wipe them clean and start all over again

- You only keep the images that you want. You can delete unwanted images immediately after you have taken them or wait until you have a chance to review all of the pictures you have taken in that session

Image editing is easy to learn and offers great possibilities for the professional and amateur alike.

- Image editing software allows you to become a picture editor and a graphic artist

- Indexing programs allow you to catalogue your images on your computer — no more boxes of pictures lying around the house

- Greater versatility in what you can do with digital images. They can be stored electronically, printed, sent around the world via email or viewed in your living room through a slide show on your television

- It is a new and rapidly advancing medium that has enormous potential for development

On the down side

However, as with every type of emerging technology, there are some drawbacks to the digital photography revolution:

Digital photography is not a cheap hobby. Once you start you will find more and more add-ons and accessories that you feel you cannot live without.

- Set-up costs. The minimum needed to produce and edit digital images is: a digital camera, a computer, editing software and a printer. The printer could be optional if you are only using images on the Web but most people would consider it a necessity. Added to this there are items such as scanners, CD writers and storage devices. On the plus side many people may have some of these items already and so they are half way there

- Printing costs. Photograph-quality paper and ink are not cheap (approximately 50 pence-£1 per A4 sheet of paper and £20 for an ink cartridge) and on top of this is the wear and tear on your printer. Some of this is offset by the fact that you will only want to print your best images and you can discard any images that are not up to scratch. Initially, it may seem that digital photography will drastically reduce your photographic processing bill, but this is not always the case. However, you will make some savings if you are using your images online

Do not be put off by the purists of the photography world who reject digital photography as a gimmick that will not last. These are the same type of people who claimed that the Internet would not catch on.

- Complexity. Some areas of digital photography can be quite daunting at first. However, a good basic grounding can be picked up reasonably quickly and the really technical aspects can quite happily be left to the techno-junkies

- Emerging technology. Digital photography is taking an increasingly firm hold in the consumer market and the development of the technology is moving very quickly. So what is cutting-edge today may seem obsolete in a year. However, if you keep waiting for the technology to advance and the prices to drop you never feel the time is right. Take the plunge now and be prepared to upgrade as time goes by. If you do, don't go back and look at the price of your equipment in six months

Using images on the Web

Digital images are ideal for emailing to friends, family and colleagues over the Web. Simply create your email, then attach the image (the Attach function is usually denoted by a paperclip icon or something similar) and send. It's as easy as that.

Web publishing

One of the main uses of digital photography is for inserting images into Web pages. This is because they can be captured at a low resolution and still maintain good quality and reasonable file size.

Digital images can be used in a variety of ways:

- On a corporate Web site — pictures to illustrate the site or the MD's happy, smiling face:

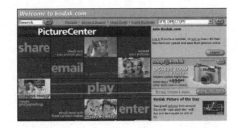

- On an internal intranet site — several companies now have employee photographs next to their names on an internal telephone directory so that everyone knows what their colleagues look like

Web users can change the settings on their browsers so that they do not show images. This saves the user time but it means that your images may not be seen.

- For use on a personal Web site — this could be used to illustrate your hobbies, promote your latest home-made gadget or show pictures of your friends and family to the cyber world:

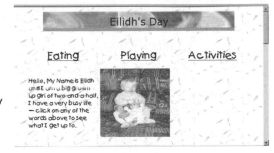

Personal Web pages are a great way to keep in touch with family and friends

With personal Web pages, you can keep your far-flung relations updated about your family by posting images on your site at regular intervals.

Web publishing rules

When you are publishing images on a Web site a few common rules apply:

- Don't overdo it. Just because you have the capability to scatter dozens of images on a single page, it does not mean you have to use it. More images mean a longer downloading time for the page and this can cause considerable frustration to the user. 'Less is more' is a good maxim to follow

- If you have to have a lot of images on one page then create them as thumbnails. These are reduced size images that can be enlarged by clicking on them:

When you put images on the Web it is possible for anyone to download them and use them as they please. It is very hard to keep track of images once they appear on the Web. So if you have a valuable image that you do not want to be copied, then do not put it on the Web.

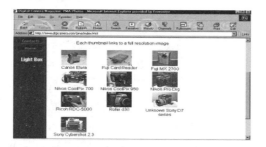

Thumbnails

- Provide a textual alternative for users who do not, or choose not to, have access to images on their browser

- Don't use images just for the sake of it. Each image should carry a powerful and pertinent message

- Don't use any images that could cause offence or distress. This is equally important whether you are creating a business Web site, an intranet site or a personal one. If in doubt, choose another image

- Never put misleading words or phrases about your images in the meta tag (the bit that is used for indexing by search engines) of your Web site. This will only annoy, frustrate or disappoint people and they may never visit your site again

Desktop publishing (DTP)

What was once thought of as an area only for professional designers is now open to anyone with a computer and a DTP package such as Adobe InDesign, Adobe PageMaker, QuarkXpress or Microsoft Publisher. These programs enable the users to create professional and high-quality items such as newsletters, magazines, brochures, reports and promotional material. Digital images can easily be incorporated into these publications and the software offers numerous options for both the layout and printing of these images.

For more details about DTP packages, visit the following Web sites:

www.adobe.com

www.quark.com

www.microsoft.com

When you are using digital images in DTP documents it is important that you know the type of printer the output device is going to be. If you are printing in-house then this should be easy to find out, but if you are dealing with a commercial printer you should do the following:

- Create a spec. sheet of exactly what you want in terms of colour, paper and photographic reproduction

- Visit the printer and discuss your requirements

- Liaise with the printer at every step of the process to make sure that it is all going well

These points are particularly important when you are using images that you want to be produced at the highest quality.

Having a DTP document produced on a colour photocopier is an effective and economical alternative to having it printed by a commercial printer. In addition, the quality of some colour photocopiers on the market today is excellent.

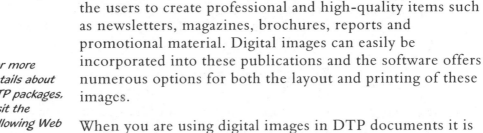

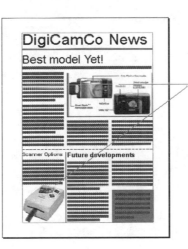

Digital images can be incorporated very successfully into documents such as newsletters. However, for the best results it is necessary to know how they are going to be printed and involve yourself in the process from start to finish

General uses

Digital photography is an excellent medium for people with young children. Most families have boxes full of photographs, some of which make it into albums or frames but most remain hidden in cupboards and drawers. With a digital camera proud parents can snap away to their heart's content and then use the best images and discard the rest.

Personal use

Digital photography can be used to provide images in much the same way as film photography would. But the digital version has many more possibilities and there are a range of options: greeting cards; calendars; business cards; invitations; and even T-shirts. You are only limited by the type of editing software you have and your imagination.

Digital photo albums

One of the great benefits of digital photography to the home user is that you can create significant photograph collections without the hassle of storing dozens of packets of photographs or albums. There are various software packages that are designed for digital image storing and cataloguing and these can give some effective results.

Two programs that offer a photo album style facility are Presto! PhotoAlbum and PhotoRecall. Their respective Web sites are: www.newsoftinc.com. and www.photorecall.com. These are useful utilities if you want to display your images in a way with which people will feel familiar.

Digital photography albums, like this one from Presto! PhotoAlbum, are an excellent way to display your images:

As well as displaying images on a computer monitor they can also be viewed on a television monitor. A cable connects the camera to the TV and then you can have a slide show instead of the weekly soap opera or feature film.

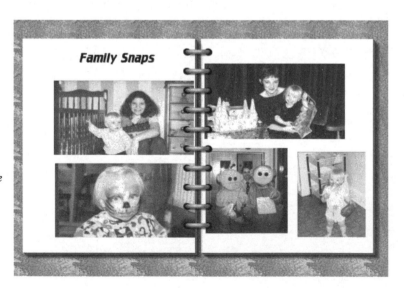

Family Snaps

Understanding pixels

The technology behind digital photography is undoubtedly complex. Although there is no need to fully understand the inner workings of a digital camera, it is important to know a bit about the overall process of creating a digital image.

Pixels: the digital building blocks

If you are involved with any form of digital imaging it will not be long before you encounter the word *pixel*. This stands for *picture element* and it is the foundation upon which every digital image is built. A pixel is a tiny square of colour and a digital image is made up of hundreds of thousands, or even millions, of these squares. If you enlarge a digital image enough it will become pixelated, which means you see each individual pixel rather than the overall image. Since pixels are so small though, once you view the image from a reasonable distance, all of the pixels merge to form (ideally) a sharp and clear image.

Using image editing software it is possible to enlarge an image and then change the colour attributes of individual pixels, if you so desire.

Each pixel represents a single colour, so for subtle colour changes it is best to have as many pixels as possible. This creates the most accurate colour representation.

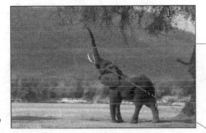

When an image is viewed 1:1 it should appear sharp

2 When it is enlarged it becomes pixelated — each individual pixel can be seen

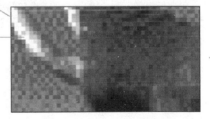

When a digital photograph is taken, the light captured by the image sensor is converted into pixels, with each pixel representing a certain colour. In general, the more pixels that you have in an image then the sharper it will appear. It is easier to get rid of extra pixels than to add new ones.

Resolution

Types of resolution

The first thing on a specification list for a digital camera is usually the resolution. This records the number of pixels in an image and can be specified in three ways: by its dimensions in pixels, i.e. 640 x 480; the total number of pixels in an image, i.e. 307,200 pixels; or pixels per inch (ppi). In general, the greater the number of pixels in an image then the better the quality. However, more pixels mean larger file sizes. The stated resolution of a digital image is not the physical size of it — this is determined by altering the image resolution in the image editing software. So an image with a resolution of 640 x 480 pixels could be displayed or printed with different dimensions, but the bigger the physical size then the poorer the quality of the image.

Some digital cameras give resolutions in interpolated values. This is a process whereby the camera adds pixels to the image. It does this by trying to match the colour, brightness, contrast and intensity of existing pixels. This increases the resolution (i.e. there are more pixels in the image) but it does not necessarily increase the quality accordingly.

Look for cameras that offer optical resolution figures i.e. the actual physical number of pixels that it is capable of capturing.

640

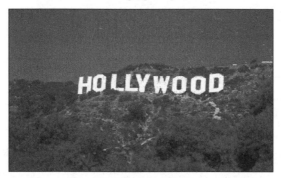

480

An image with a resolution of 640 x 480 pixels (not the physical dimensions)

Most entry level digital cameras have a minimum resolution of 640 x 480 pixels. The next step up is cameras that offer a resolution in the region of 1200 x 800 pixels (or 1 million in total) and these are known as megapixel cameras. There are also multimegapixel cameras which can capture over 2 million pixels. Understandably, the price of the camera increases with the number of pixels that it can capture but it is worth going for the best one you can afford.

Image resolution

When it comes to outputting an image, the resolution in terms of pixels per inch is the important consideration. A lot of digital cameras automatically save images at 72–96 ppi. This means that if the image was viewed on a monitor or printed on paper there would be 72 or 96 pixels in each linear inch. So if the number of pixels in the image was 1200 wide and 900 high (the resolution of a mid-range digital camera) then this image could be produced at a size of 12.5 inches by 9.4 inches (1200 divided by 96 and 900 divided by 96). The final quality of the image will depend on the type of output device that is being used.

Resizing an image

The resolution of an image can be set from within the image editing software. Once this has been done the resolution remains the same, regardless of the type of output device being used.

In most editing packages, when you change the resolution of an image this does not affect the on- screen view. If you want to change this you can do so by changing the magnification or, in some programs, the canvas size.

Also, changing the image resolution does not change the size of the file, it just means that the pixels will be closer together or further apart when printed.

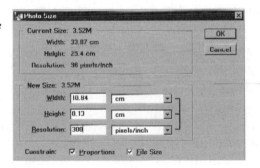

Changing the resolution of an image in an editing program alters the size at which it will be output

Changing the resolution of an image changes the size at which it will appear once it is printed or viewed on screen. If, in the example in the first paragraph, the image resolution was 300 ppi then the image would be output at a size of 4 inches by 3 inches (1200 divided by 300 and 900 divided by 300).

The size of images can also be changed by using a process called resampling. This involves the software adding more pixels to the image using a method of electronic guess work. This creates a bigger image but with lower quality.

Outputting images

The issue of resolution becomes important when you want to display your images because it affects the size at which they can be viewed satisfactorily. The two main areas are displaying on the Web and printing hard copy.

Of the two, using images on the Web is the more straightforward. Most computer monitors display images at 72 or 96 ppi so an image that has a resolution of 640 x 480 pixels can be viewed at a size of approximately 9 inches by 6.5 inches. (This is calculated by dividing 640 and 480 by 72.) If you want a larger image then the quality will decrease slightly because each pixel will have to increase in size to cover the extra area.

A printed image will always look better on high quality photographic paper than standard multi-copy paper. Bear this in mind when you are viewing your printed images.

When digital images are printed as hard copy the same calculation can be applied — the dimensions of the image (in pixels) divided by the resolution set in the image editing software. The best image resolution setting for colour inkjet printers is 300 ppi as this gives the best output quality. So to print an image with the dimensions of 640 x 480 at a resolution of 300 ppi the resulting size would be:

640/300 = 2.13 inches

by

480/300 = 1.6 inches

Even though some printers have an output resolution of up to 1440 dots per inch (dpi), always work with 300 ppi as the optimum print resolution.

By anyone's standards this is small for a printed photograph. You can increase the size by setting your image resolution to 72, but this would result in a lower quality of picture because 72 coloured dots in an inch are a lot less tightly packed than 300. So if you want to take digital images for printing hard copy then go for a camera with as high a resolution as your budget can stretch to.

The best way to see how printers handle digital images is to get a demonstration from a retailer. If possible take one of your own images for them to use rather than the pre-installed ones in the shop. This way you will see a truer result for your own needs rather than relying on an image that is designed to show the printer in its best light.

A whole book could be written on the topic of pixels and resolution, and they have been, but the main points to remember are:

Resolution is a popular term in the imaging world and is also used in relation to monitors and printers. Make sure you know what is being referred to when you hear the word resolution.

- The more pixels in an image then the better the quality will be from the output device

- When calculating the physical size of your image, divide the number of pixels across (or down) by the image resolution set within the image editing program

- For images that are going to be displayed on the Web, set the image resolution to 72 or 96 (ppi)

- For images that are going to be printed, set the image resolution to 300 (ppi)

- Image resolution can be altered in the editing software

- The higher the resolution then the larger the file

For an in-depth look at resolution, pixels and most other aspects of digital imaging, take a look at:

www.shortcourses.com

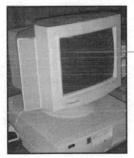

1 If an image is being viewed on a monitor then the size it can best be displayed at can be calculated by setting the image resolution to 72 or 96 (the resolution of the monitor)

2 If an image is being printed then the output size can be calculated by setting the image resolution to 300 (the ideal resolution for the printer)

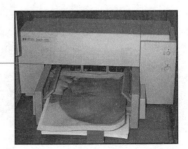

Image compression

One of the most popular photographic file formats, JPEG (Joint Photographic Expert Group) has been designed so that it handles compression well. This means that it produces good quality images while maintaining small file sizes.

Most digital cameras offer a variety of compression settings when an image is being captured. This involves creating a smaller sized image file by discarding some of the pixels that the camera decides are superfluous. This inevitably leads to some loss of image quality but it does mean that more images can be stored when you are taking pictures. Typically, digital cameras have compression settings along the lines of Good, Better, Best. These refer to the final quality of the image — Good is the most compression, Best the least.

The amount of compression used will depend on what the image is going to be used for:

- An image for a Web site does not have to be of a high resolution so this can be taken on maximum compression

- A image that is going to be printed as a hard copy will be required to be of the best resolution available and so minimal or no compression should be used

A newer file format, PNG (Portable Network Graphics), is similar to JPEGs but is not as widely used.

Although the idea of compression sounds like a drawback as far as the quality of printed images is concerned this is not necessarily the case. With the naked eye the quality of a moderately compressed image is little different to that of one with no compression. In addition, compressing images can be useful if you are taking some preliminary shots to gain the best angle or view of a subject.

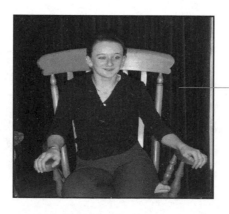

When taking portraits it is a good idea to take some introductory shots so that both the photographer and subject feel comfortable. These can be done using maximum compression

Colours in digital images

The colour in a digital image is based on the RGB (Red, Green, Blue) colour model. This is the method of creating colours that is used by both digital cameras and computer monitors (and also devices such as televisions). To achieve the colour that the human eye sees, a RGB device mixes red, green and blue to produce the final multi-coloured image. This can produces images with up to approximately 16 million colours in them.

As far as capturing a digital image is concerned it is enough to know that RGB is the colour model that digital cameras use. However, it comes into its own when the image editing software takes over. With these programs you can alter the levels of RGB in an image. This allows for considerable subtlety in the editing process.

In top of the range image editing programs, the RGB model is broken up into the individual colour, also know as colour channels. Each channel can then be edited independently of each other.

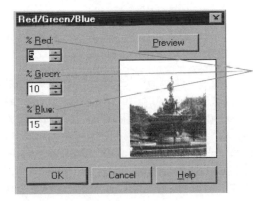

Some editing programs allow for the individual Red, Green and Blue colour channels to be edited independently of each other

Although digital cameras and computer monitors use the RGB colour model, printers (unfortunately from a simplicity point-of-view) use the CMYK (Cyan, Magenta, Yellow, Black) colour model. This is because most colour printers are not able to reproduce all of the colours that the RGB model can since ink is not as pure as natural light. Therefore black (the K in the CMYK colour model — not B in case people confuse this for blue) is used to create pure black and also correct any colour variations. As far as converting a RGB image into a CMYK hard copy is concerned, this is usually taken care of by the printer software.

Colour depth

The final quality of the colour in a digital image depends on the number of *bits* that are used to make up each pixel. A bit (short for binary digit) is the electronic representation of either 0 or 1, also known as binary code, which is a language universally understood by computers. Each bit in a pixel is used to store important data about the colour of that pixel: the more bits, the more information stored and so the final image is of a higher quality.

When calculating file size, it is worth remembering the basics of file measurements:

- *8 bits = 1 byte*
- *1,024 bytes = 1 kilobyte (1K)*
- *1,024 kilobytes = 1 megabyte (1Mb)*
- *1.024 megabytes = 1 gigabyte (1 Gb)*

The number of bits used to make up a pixel of colour is known as the *bit depth* and there are two main choices:

- 8-bit, which gives a total number of colours of 256. This means that each pixel is made up of 8 bits. The figure of 256 is arrived at because since each bit can be either 0 or 1 the total number is 2 to the power of 8, which is 256

- 24-bit, which gives a total number of 16.7 million colour combinations (2 to the power of 24)

The higher the bit depth of the image then the larger the size of the image file, since each bit takes up room in the file. Therefore file formats that are designed for specific purposes have different bit depths: a GIF file, which is used for Web graphics, is an 8-bit (256 colours) format while a JPEG format (which is also used for Web images, but specifically photographic ones) is a 24-bit (16 million colour) format. When you are considering colour depth, you will have to decide whether you want the highest colour quality possible and a larger file, or a slightly inferior colour quality and a smaller file.

A 256 colour image creates a file size of approximately one third less than a 16 million colour one. This varies between different file formats.

The colour depth of an image does not affect the number of pixels that are used to make it up: a 24-bit image with 1 million pixels, still has the same number if it is displayed as an 8-bit image. However, the 24-bit version will result in a much larger file.

It is possible to have a higher colour depth than 24-bit but this is the level at which most computer software and output devices currently operate most efficiently.

Equipping yourself

Knowing what you need to take effective digital photographs can be a daunting prospect at first. This chapter shows you the equipment that you will need and some of the areas to consider when you are buying it.

Covers

Chapter Two

Looking at digital cameras

At first sight the range of digital cameras is both dazzling and bewildering. Some of them look like conventional compact or SLR cameras, while others resemble something out of a science fiction series. As yet there is no standardised design for digital cameras so the first thing to say is, forget what it looks like, make a close inspection of what it does. If it looks sleek and shiny, but does not do the job you want it to, then move on to another model.

Digital cameras are generally quite light — but don't let this give you the impression that they are insignificant. There is a lot of technology packed into that light body.

Digital cameras range in price from under £100 to some staggering sums in the region of £20,000. There is something for every level of digital photographer; from the casual image taker to the professional snapper. Before taking the plunge it is important to ascertain what it is you are going to be using a digital camera for. Some of the options include:

• Capturing images for display on Web pages

• Using images for business presentations, with a presentation package such as PowerPoint

• Printing medium-quality snapshots

• Printing high-quality prints

• Creating publication-quality DTP documents

Digital cameras are prime candidates for retailers who like to push extended warranties with their products. If you do want this type of service it is usually cheaper to get it from a specialist insurance company.

Each of these options will require a different specification from the camera. For Web images, and on-screen presentations, an entry level model would suffice (although you may want a higher specification if you are going to print your business presentation in hard copy) while the higher the print quality you require, then the more advanced the camera will need to be.

It is easy to become dazzled by the sheer volume of gadgetry associated with digital cameras. The devices themselves are beguiling objects and it is possible to let your heart rule your credit card when it comes to buying one. Before you make a choice, take some time to assess your needs in relation to the options on offer.

It's more than just a camera.

When you buy a digital camera you will discover that it consists of a lot more than the camera itself. There will also be:

When you buy a digital camera, check all of the cables so you know what they are all for.

- Cables to connect it to a computer. These can be used to connect the camera to the computer once the camera software has been installed. This enables the camera and the computer to communicate with each other

- Some form of transfer device to get the images into the computer. In some models this is done by connecting the two devices by cables. However, in more recent models this has been superseded by memory card readers of various descriptions or even infrared transmission

Some digital imaging accessories are actually essential while others are nice to have. Get the important ones first and then indulge yourself at a later date.

- Software to edit the images and, in some cases, software to create Web pages. The standard of these is usually proportionate to the price of the camera but even the entry-level models have software that is perfectly adequate for general image editing

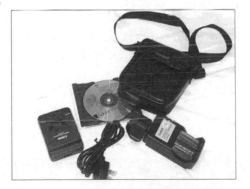

Digital photography uses a variety of accessories, some of which are essential and others which are desirable

All of the above are important for the overall imaging process so it is worth examining closely what different models offer. Discuss with your retailer the pros and cons of various models and if they are not prepared to spend time with you then go somewhere else.

Researching the options

Because of the diverse range of digital cameras on offer, and the different uses for them, it is essential to do some research into the subject before venturing off to dispense your hard earned cash. If you walk into a computer or photography shop with little knowledge of the options available then you may come out with a very expensive mistake.

Luckily there is plenty of help at hand when looking into the varied world of digital cameras:

- Camera magazines. Traditional photography magazines are slowly beginning to realise that digital photography is here to stay and more features on this area are starting to appear. In addition, they are also useful for general photography tips which can be applied equally well to digital photography

- Computer magazines. General computer magazines frequently carry articles on digital photography including reviews of new products. It is best to read at least two or three different publications so that you get as balanced a view as possible

- Consumer magazines. Magazines such as Which? and Which Camera? periodically review the latest digital products and it could be worth keeping an eye out for these. They have Web sites at www.which.com and www.whichcamera.co.uk respectively, although there is a subscription fee for some services. Most large libraries carry back copies and also indices of subjects that have been covered

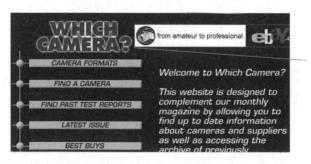

Several popular consumer magazines also have online versions

Another source of information about digital photography is from *Newsgroups on the Internet. These are groups of like-minded individuals who communicate with each other on the Internet. There are thousands of these Newsgroups, covering a multitude of subjects. It is free to join a Newsgroup and you can either see what everyone else has to say or add your own comments.*

Contact your Internet Service Provider for more details.

- The Internet. The Web is an ideal source of information on digital imaging. A good way to start is to enter 'digital photography' or 'digital imaging' into an Internet search engine. There are several online magazines that offer up-to-date news and reviews. Some Web sites to try are www.pcphotomag.com, www.digicamera.com and www.zdnet.com/pcmag (this is a general PC magazine but it carries a lot of digital imaging features). Also, the Web sites of companies such as Kodak (www.kodak.com), Olympus (www.olympus.com) and Nikon (www.nikon.com) have general digital imaging information and product details

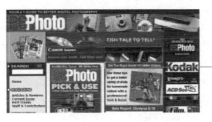

There are several Web sites specifically for digital camera users

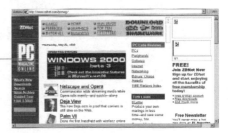

2 General PC sites also carry information on imaging products

- Professional camera/computer stores. The key word here is *professional*. You should be able to walk into a shop selling digital cameras and get an informed view of the subject without a hard sell sales pitch. In general, smaller specialist shops are more willing to take the time explaining the subject than the larger electronics stores. When you are actually buying a camera, ask to test all of the models in which you are interested

Considering computers

PC or Apple Mac?

Thankfully the long-running question of compatibility between PCs and the Apple Mac is one that does not need to overly concern the digital photographer. Digital camera manufacturers are well aware of this potential conflict and most devices are compatible with both types of machine. In some cases you may need special cables to connect to a Mac but there will be software available for the two systems. If in doubt, ask your retailer.

Digital images can usually be viewed in either PC or Mac format. Most digital image formats are compatible with both platforms so they can be shared between the two.

If you already own a computer then there is no great need to worry about compatibility issues, just double-check when you are buying a camera. If you are buying a new computer then it is a matter of personal choice. Macs have traditionally been the favoured platform for designers and graphic artists and they are well equipped to handle complicated image editing. After several years in the commercial doldrums, Apple has made something of a revival, based largely on its multi-coloured iMac range. Alternatively, PCs are used by approximately 90% of computer users and so there is a wider range of software and accessories available. If you want safety in numbers then go for a PC; if you want to assert your individuality then a Mac is perhaps the way to go.

Processor speed

It is a generally accepted fact in the computer world that what is a lightening fast processor today will be a deadly slow one tomorrow. To run most image editing software a minimum of a good quality 486 chip (or Mac equivalent) is usually required. However, this is something of a dinosaur in the computing world and you should really be looking at a Pentium chip as a starting point. Once you start editing images you will soon realise it can take a reasonably long time for editing changes to be applied to even a moderately small image.

However, processor speed is not the only consideration when considering your computer's ability to process and store information.

RAM and ROM

The two types of computer memory, RAM (Random Access Memory) and ROM (Read Only Memory), are important to the digital editor for different reasons. The amount of RAM affects how quickly the computer will be able to process the image when it is being edited and the amount of ROM will determine the storage capabilities of the computer, for both the editing software and the completed images.

Buying extra RAM for a computer has dropped in price dramatically in recent years. What was once considered a major purchase can now be bought for approximately £1 per Mb.

If you ask anyone who works with computers for the single most valuable upgrade for their system the chances are they will say RAM. It is fair to say that you can never have too much RAM, particularly if you are doing a lot of image editing, which can consume large chunks of this valuable commodity. The amount of RAM not only affects the processing speed of your computer, it can also determine whether the machine crashes at regular intervals or not. If a computer is struggling for memory when processing an image it may decide to give up the challenge.

ROM is the memory on the computer's hard drive, which is used to store files and also the software that is put on the system. Some modern consumer computers come with enormous quantities of ROM — up to a staggering 80 Gb (gigabyte) in some cases. While it is unlikely that you will fill up that much in a short space of time it is nonetheless worthwhile trying to have as much hard disc memory as possible. There are two reasons for this:

If you are confident about examining the insides of your computer then it is reasonably easy to insert extra RAM yourself. However, if you feel unsure then take it to a specialist computer shop. If you do install it yourself it may invalidate your original warranty.

- As you do more digital photography it is inevitable that you will want to add more software to your system and image editing software is invariably memory-hungry

- The more you experiment with digital images, the more you will acquire. Imagine if all of the photos lying around the house were to be transferred to your computer. Before long your hard drive will start filling up and there may come a point when you will want to investigate some of the storage devices looked at later in this chapter

Monitor size

When you are doing a lot of image editing work the size and quality of monitor can become an issue. If you are using a 14–16 inch screen, which comes as standard with many computers, you may find that after a period of time you are straining to see your work. Also, if you are working with several different toolbars then these may take up a considerable amount of your editing space. If possible, go for a 17 inch monitor or higher. These cost in the range of £200 upwards for a SVGA model and your eyes may consider it a good investment.

Some image editing software can calibrate your monitor so that the colour on screen is as close to the printed version as possible.

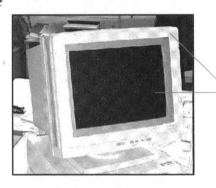

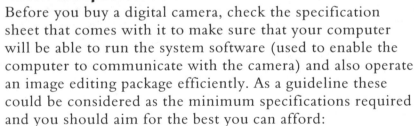

If you are going to be doing a lot of image editing then a large monitor and a glare guard are essential

Check the specification

As you do more and more image processing, you will begin to crave a faster and more powerful system. This is a fact of computing life and it is a condition that never goes away.

Before you buy a digital camera, check the specification sheet that comes with it to make sure that your computer will be able to run the system software (used to enable the computer to communicate with the camera) and also operate an image editing package efficiently. As a guideline these could be considered as the minimum specifications required and you should aim for the best you can afford:

•   486/66 processor, 32 Mb RAM, up to 2 Gb of ROM (or the equivalent for an Apple Mac).

If you can afford it, then aim for at least a Pentium processor and 64 Mb of RAM. Also, you may think that 2 Gb of ROM is plenty but you will soon fill it up when you start adding software and your images. And, as with most things associated with computers it is always nice to have that little bit extra, just in case.

Choosing a printer

Once the work of capturing, processing and editing a digital image has been completed it is time to look for an output device. If the image is being displayed on the Web then this solves the problem — the image merely has to be inserted into a suitable format and then published on the Web. During the whole operation the image never leaves the safe environment of the computer.

As well as the printers there are also print consumables such as paper and ink to consider.

However, if you want to have a printed image of your endeavours, as most people do at some time, then you will need some form of printing device for outputting your image. Although the market for printing digital images is dominated by one type of printer, there are several options from which to choose:

- Inkjet printers. By far the most common type of colour printer for digital images. Inkjet printers are relatively cheap, easy to use and, given the right circumstances, can produce excellent near photographic quality. The technology in this area is improving all the time and the output quality is getting better and better

Lexmark, the printer makers, have developed a printer that accepts both CompactFlash and SmartMedia memory cards. They are slotted into the printer and the images can then be printed. This is a considerable innovation because it allows for printed images without the need for a computer.

- Laser printers. Colour laser printers produce good results but they are expensive. Business use is the best bet for this type of printer

- Dye-sublimation printers. This type of printer produces a continuous tone image by welding coloured dyes onto the paper by a heat process. It is generally accepted that dye-sublimation printers produce the closest results to actual photographic quality. Their one main drawback is that they can only be used for colour printing, so you would need a separate printer for your textual printing needs. It is likely that this type of printer will become more and more popular in the near future

- Micro dry printers. These printers use a similar process to dye-sublimation printers but using an ink coated ribbon instead of dyes. Can also print text

Removable memory options

An efficient way of storing and transferring images is to use a camera that has some form of removable memory, as opposed to on-board memory. This comes in four types:

- CompactFlash

- SmartMedia

- Floppy disc

- PC cards

The type of removable memory will depend on the model of camera but the first two are the best options in terms of size and storage capacity.

A floppy disc has the advantage that it can be taken out of the camera and inserted straight into the computer floppy drive. On the downside a limit of 2 Mb of storage space can be very restricting when taking digital images — a high quality image could easily be three times the size of a floppy disc.

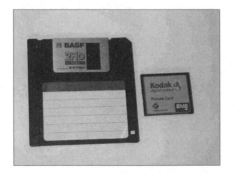

Floppy discs are much bigger than CompactFlash cards, but the latter hold a lot more data

Both CompactFlash and SmartMedia cards can be bought containing varying amounts of memory. However, they are not cheap and cost in the region of £2 per Mb. This is the one drawback to what is the easiest and most efficient way of capturing and storing images. And, despite the initial cost, these devices are relatively economical since they can be reused numerous times. However, they are very small and delicate so take good care of them.

Assessing transfer devices

Once you have captured your images onto your camera's memory, you will need some method of transferring them onto the computer. There are three options available: cable transfer, infrared transfer and card adapters as discussed on the facing page. Before you begin transferring any data, make sure you have installed the system software that comes with the camera. This will enable the computer and the camera to communicate with each other during the downloading process.

On some computers the cable connection is through a USB (Universal Serial Bus) port which speeds up the downloading time considerably. Newer computers are usually fitted with USB ports.

Cable transfer

This method is used most frequently if a camera has some form of on-board memory. However, it can also be used if there is a removable storage device in the camera, such as a disc of some type. To conduct this method of transfer a cable is attached to the camera and a COM port (on a PC) or into the printer or modem port (on a Mac) at the back of the computer. The data is transmitted through the cable into the computer. However, this has two main drawbacks;

- It is slow

- It can be irritating to have to fumble around with yet more cables at the back of the computer every time you want to download images

It can be a frustrating and time-consuming business adjusting all of the settings for infrared downloading. Make sure you follow all of the instructions in the user manual and be patient.

Infrared transfer

This is a relatively new development in the field of image transfer which requires the camera to have an infrared transceiver and the computer to have an infrared port. Devices which can communicate with each other via infrared signals are known as IrDA (Infrared Data Association) compliant devices.

If your camera and computer are IrDA compliant then you can download your images by placing the camera facing the computer's infrared transceiver and downloading your data. Although this method does away with the need for more cables it operates at a similar speed to cable transfer. However, it offers a bit of oneupmanship if you can tell your friends you download by infrared.

Image editing software

Technically, it would be possible to capture digital images and print them out without ever introducing image editing software into the equation. However, you would not be able to amend or manipulate your images, so one of the main assets of digital photography would be lost.

Image editing software allows you to edit the colour attributes of an image, add your own text or graphics, apply touch-up techniques and incorporate them into designs such as greeting cards, gift tags or posters.

The bad news about imaging software is that it can cost up to £500 for the most sophisticated programs. But the good news is that there are numerous entry level programs for approximately £50 that give an excellent introduction to the subject. Even better, all digital cameras come with some type of imaging software. Some even come with the top-of-the-range packages.

Professional programs

The accepted market-leader for professional image editors is Adobe Photoshop. This does everything you could ever want from an imaging package and more besides. However, for the novice it can be quite daunting to use and is best suited to people who have some prior experience of the digital imaging world. Having said that, there is certainly nothing to touch it as far as versatility, functionality and quality are concerned.

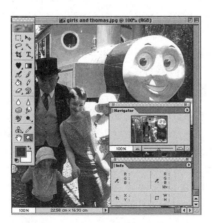

Programs such as Adobe Photoshop or Photoshop Elements are excellent for image editing, but at first sight they can be a confusing collection of menus, toolbars and icons

Entry-level programs offer every assistance during the editing process. Take some time exploring the Help features and going through the online tutorials.

Entry-level programs

While entry-level imaging programs do not offer the finesse of their professional cousins, a lot of users will not miss these subtleties. A lot of less expensive programs still offer colour controls, special effects and touch up techniques. With very little experience it is possible to create digitally enhanced images that will have people thinking that you have been doing it for years.

The great advantage of these programs is that they are very user friendly and guide the novice user through the whole process of digital imaging with the aid of icons, help assistants, templates and wizards.

Another feature is the uses you can make of your images with these programs. In addition to merely enhancing them you will be able to create cards, posters and invitations incorporating your favourite images and also email them to friends and family via your image-editing program. With some programs you can also create slide shows, print images for T-shirts or design your very own personalised mug. The emphasis with these programs is to make image editing as easy and hassle-free as possible. But most of the programs still manage to pack in an enormous number of functions.

In some entry level programs the editing functions are controlled by selecting the effect that you want through an icon and then dragging and dropping it into the image to be edited.

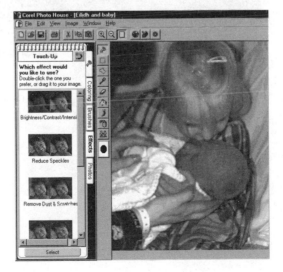

An entry-level editing package, such as Corel Photo House, offers a variety of editing options within an easy-to-use interface

Fun packages

Digital photography is supposed to be fun and some programs take this to extremes by allowing images to have numerous special effects applied to them. This can include distorting images so that they resemble bizarre caricatures or creating patterns by duplicating images, or merging items from different images to create your own e-fit image from parts of your family and friends.

The technical side of these programs involves shifting the pixels in the image around like shifting sand around in a sandpit. The practical side is that it can be a lot of fun for everyone:

Fun packages are an excellent way to produce photographic caricatures. However, do not overdo the distortion to the point where it becomes over-the-top.

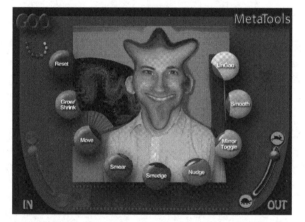

Special effects editing packages can produce amusing, if somewhat unflattering, images

Three fun orientated imaging packages include Kai's SuperGoo, Professor Franklin's Instant Photo Effects and LivePix Deluxe.

Fun packages such as this one are ideal for children for the following reasons:

- They give a good introduction to basic computer techniques

- They are fun and easy to use, while still stimulating creative instincts

- They are ideal for wet holiday days when the kids are getting fed up!

Storage devices

As you collect more and more digital images there will probably come a point when you will want to store them on something other than your computer's hard drive. There are two reasons for this:

Standard 100 MB Zip drives should cost between £75-£100. The discs cost approximately £10 each. It should be possible to obtain a reasonable discount if they are bought in bulk.

- Purely for back-up, in case your hard drive fails

- In order to free up space on your hard drive for your other computing needs

Floppy discs

Most computer users are familiar with floppy discs. They are cheap, straightforward to use and relatively robust. But for digital images they are not ideal. This is because they only hold a maximum of 2 Mb of data. This is enough to hold a few low resolution, high compression images but for anything much bigger they are too small.

Zip drives

If your computer only has one parallel port and your printer is already connected to it, you can cable the printer through the Zip drive. Detach the printer cable and attach it to the connector at the back of the Zip drive. Then connect the Zip cable to the computer's parallel port.

One of the success stories of computer storage in recent years has been the Zip drive. This is similar to a floppy disc drive, except that the discs hold 100 Mb of data. This is for the standard model and there are options that offer up to 1 Gb of storage. Zip drives can be internal and external. The external version is connected with standard cabling to a parallel port at the back of the computer. A recent addition to this range is a 250 Mb Zip drive. This can also read 100 MB disks, but the 100 Mb drive cannot read the 250 Mb discs.

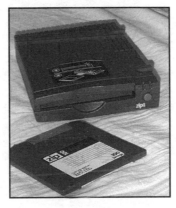

Zip drives can be used in the same way as a floppy drive, with files being copied to it via your hard drive. However, they hold a minimum of 100 Mb of data

CD-ROMs

CD-ROMs offer 650 Mb of data storage and this option is becoming increasingly popular. Images on CD-ROMs can either be created by a professional bureau or you can create your own using a CD writer. This is a device that transfers images (among other items) from your computer onto a CD-ROM. This is an area that is developing quickly and is becoming more and more popular with users. At present CD writers cost in the region of £100 upwards.

CD writers come in both internal and external varieties. The type that you choose may depend on your ability to fit it internally and the amount of space on your desktop.

Initially it may appear that a CD's 650 Mbs of storage space is an enormous amount and you will only ever need one CD. But while a CD has approximately 430 times the storage space of a humble floppy disc, you will be amazed at how quickly you fill one up. As your digital photography repertoire expands so will your collection of images. It is a harsh fact of computer storage life that there is no such thing as too much storage capacity.

One important issue with creating your own CDs is format. Some CDs can be copied as read-only (CD-R) which means you cannot erase any data from them and you cannot reuse them once they are full. The other format is rewritable (CD-RW) which means you can delete or copy over items that are already on the disc. This gives you more versatility but there is also the risk that you could record over an image that you wanted to keep. Also, since CD-RWs have come onto the market more recently, some older CD-ROM drives cannot read them.

It is highly likely that, in time, CDs will replace floppy discs as the standard type of storage disc. This is already happening in some cases — the Apple iMac does not have a floppy disc drive at all.

Archiving images

Just as hard copy images fade over time, so too do digitally stored ones. The best way to preserve your images is on a CD. The CD-R variety is the best bet here because it gives images an approximate shelf life of 100 years, as opposed to a third of that for CD-RW.

CDs are an excellent way to save and keep your images. Don't underestimate the importance of this — in 100 years time your descendants will appreciate the fact that you took the trouble to archive your images.

Accessories

If you are one of those people who believe you will never get caught up in the giddy world of accessories and peripherals, then think again. Digital photography is a magnet for add-ons and extra gadgets and in this respect it could give the computing world a run for its money. Some of the items that you may want to consider to satisfy your craving for more gizmos are:

- A camera bag. This could be seen as a necessity rather than an accessory (when you start thinking like this then you know you really are hooked). If you have bought a delicate piece of technology for several hundred pounds then it makes sense to try and keep it as secure as possible. Some models come with their own bags, but if you want something a bit sturdier then try a specialist camera shop

It you are going to be using a tripod a lot it is a good investment to buy a sturdy one. They can undergo a fair amount of wear and tear during normal photographic duties.

- A tripod. A standard piece of equipment for some photographers, while other do not consider it necessary for their type of photography. As a rule, if you would use one for traditional photography, then do so for the digital variety

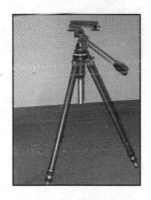

A good quality tripod is a worthwhile investment for a digital photographer. The best way to test them is to press down on the neck of the tripod. If it remains firm and stable then it should be sturdy enough for most uses

Memory cards can be bought in a variety of sizes, from 4 Mb to a colossal 192 Mb.

- Extra memory cards. At least one card is usually supplied with the camera but it is always a good idea to have a spare one. This can come in useful if your working card becomes full or damaged. Prices vary but a 16 Mb card costs in the region of £40.

If you invest in a battery charger then you will save a lot of money on new batteries. However, it still costs money to recharge the batteries and this can take up to eight hours for a standard charger. High-end chargers can do the job in half that time.

- A battery charger and rechargeable batteries. As soon as you start using a camera with an LCD (Liquid Crystal Display) you will realise the importance of a battery charger. These mini screens use up batteries at an enormous rate and a recharger could save you from buying batteries by the truck load. Even so, always make sure you carry at least one spare set of batteries with you

- Additional lenses. With some digital cameras it is possible to get lens attachments, such as you would fit on a standard SLR (Single Lens Reflex) camera. These include close up lenses, wide angle lenses and telephoto lenses

- Cleaning equipment. It is good practice to clean your camera and it will certainly not do it any harm. One simple but useful item is a lint-free cloth. This can be used to clean the LCD panel, which has a habit of smearing easily

If you are well and truly bitten by the accessory bug then it will be a costly habit and one that is hard to break. But at the same time, it will give you a lot of fun.

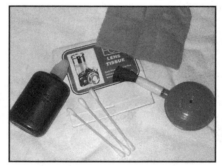

Cleaning equipment can include a lint-free cloth, a lens cleaner, an airbrush, cotton buds and cleaning fluid

Buying accessories

It pays to shop around for all items related to digital photography and this is particularly so with accessories. Due to the nature of the medium these are now appearing in photographic shops, computer shops and also general electrical shops. Look for the best price and also the best service. If you can build up a good relationship with a retailer of digital accessories then this may come in useful in the future.

Buying a digital camera

This chapter sets out some of the things to look for when you are buying a digital camera. It also shows how digital and film photography share some common elements.

Covers

Chapter Three

Price and range

Range and price

One of the main barriers to the widespread use of digital cameras is price. For the equivalent of a medium range digital machine you would be able to buy a very high specification film camera instead. However, the technology behind digital imaging is improving constantly and digital cameras are destined to fall dramatically in price in the months and years to come. Already there have been some considerable drops in prices — some cameras have fallen by nearly 50% in the space of a year and this is the type of price drop that can be expected to continue.

If you want to make a guess about how digital cameras will develop in the next few years, take a look at the world of the personal computer: the prices keep falling while the technology keeps improving.

As with all emerging technology it is hard to provide precise and lasting price comparisons, but as a general guideline a reasonable budget digital camera costs between £100–£300, medium range models are £500–£1000 and top of the line and professional models can be anything up to £20,000.

Some features to look for on a digital camera are:

*   The type of lens

*   The control functions

*   The method of connection to the computer

Some digital cameras also double up as Webcams, which can be used to send pictures and video over the Internet. One such model is the Kodak EZ200 which costs £100 and, for the price, does a decent job on both fronts.
Most digital cameras currently made by Agfa also operate as Webcams.

*   The software that is provided

Basic models

Some entry level camera can be bought for as little as £100, and the quality of these has improved markedly in only the last couple of years. However, for two or three times this price you will be able to pick up a very good budget model. This will most likely offer a minimum resolution of 640 x 480 pixels, which is perfectly adequate if you just want to use images on a Web site or email them to people. Although this level of resolution is currently the standard for entry-level cameras, the advances being made in this area suggest that it may not be too long before this is considered the dodo of digital imaging.

Megapixel cameras

Digital cameras that have a resolution of at least 1200 x 800 pixels (over 1 million pixels in total) are often referred to as megapixel cameras. This is the range that has the strongest foothold in the consumer market and it is the level that should be looked at for anyone who is considering a digital camera to produce printed images. Most of the main camera manufacturers — Nikon, Kodak, Canon, Olympus, Fuji and Agfa — have a range of megapixel cameras, as do IT or electronics orientated organisations such as Hewlett Packard, Sony, Sanyo and Casio. When comparing cameras it is advisable not to get too hung up over a few pixels of resolution: depending on its design, a camera with a 1280 x 960 resolution may produce a better image than one with a higher specification.

When you are buying a camera ask the retailer to explain the details of the camera's resolution. If they just say, 'Well, it's a megapixel model' and nothing else, then look elsewhere.

Some megapixel models, such as the Nikon CoolPix 950 and 990 have swivel heads that can rotate around the body of the camera. This can be useful for capturing shots in inaccessible positions.

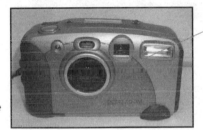

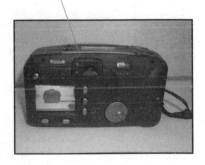

The front and back of a megapixel camera, in this case the Kodak DC 240

Multimegapixel

Cameras that are capable of capturing over 2 million pixels in total are grouped together under the multimegapixel label. This means that they are high quality and expensive. When this group starts falling in price then it will open up a whole new avenue for the digital image maker. The image quality of these machines is high but a certain level of photographic knowledge is required in order for them to operate at their full capacity.

The functions of a digital camera

Some digital cameras have different design features from standard film cameras. However, many of the functions and elements are similar (this example is a Kodak DC 3400):

Self-timer light   Light sensor   Viewfinder

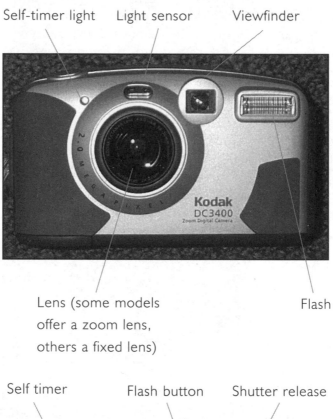

Viewfinders on digital cameras do not usually have a lot of information displayed in them. In most cases this is on the Status display on the top of the camera.

Lens (some models offer a zoom lens, others a fixed lens)

Flash

Self timer   Flash button   Shutter release

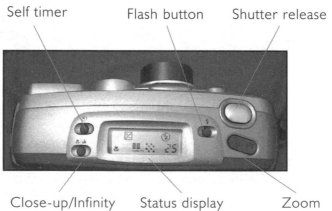

Close-up/Infinity   Status display   Zoom

Menu button   Ready lights   Viewfinder   Power

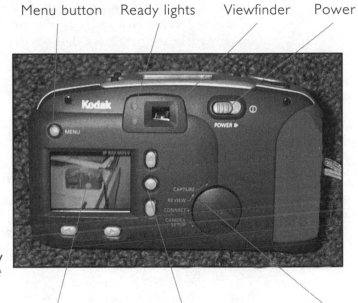

*As far as the
LCD panel is
concerned, the
bigger the
better. This will
give you a good idea of what
the final version of the
image will look like.*

LCD panel   Menu control   Camera settings,
                buttons   including Capture,
                                  Review, Connect
                                  and Setup

Memory card slot

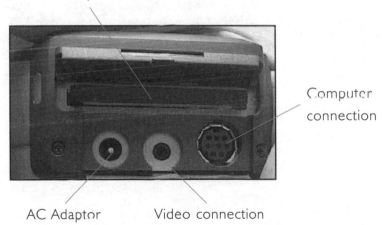

Computer
connection

AC Adaptor   Video connection

The workings of a digital camera

Although you would need a degree in camera and computer technology to explain every last detail of how a digital camera works, a little basic knowledge can be useful. Some people are interested in what goes on behind the scenes, while for others it is enough that it works when you press the required buttons.

The majority of consumer-level digital cameras do not offer a great deal of flexibility for setting the shutter speed manually. This means it can be difficult if you want to use it for techniques such as capturing fast moving objects by freezing the action.

Aperture and shutter speed

The traditional way that cameras have controlled the exposure of an image, i.e. the amount of light that falls onto the film, is to vary the aperture and the shutter speed. The aperture determines how much light gets into the camera, and the shutter speed determines the length of time it has to make an impact on the film. Aperture is measured in f-stops — the smaller the number, i.e. f2, then the more light that is allowed to pass through the lens.

Shutter speed is measured in fractions of a second. A standard shutter speed is 1/125th of a second, which is the length of time that the shutter is open to allow light to pass through onto the film. Shutter speed and aperture can be combined to give different end results on traditional film.

On a lot of entry-level digital cameras the exposure is determined by the length of time that the diodes on the image sensor are activated for receiving light. Although this differs from the method employed by film cameras, the exposure settings on digital cameras are expressed in f-numbers for aperture and divisions of a second for shutter speeds. These are the equivalent values and this is to ensure uniformity between the two mediums.

On some digital cameras the exposure is set automatically so you do not have to worry about it. However, always try and make sure there is the option to set your own controls if needed.

When dealing with aperture and shutter speed settings on a digital camera the important points to remember are:

*   Although the terminology is technically different, the digital values are given in equivalent terms

*   Settings are usually set automatically by the camera unless you change the exposure settings

Film speed

Since digital cameras do not have films they do not have a film speed classification as traditional cameras and films do. This is expressed in terms of an ISO number and is most commonly in the range of 100–400. The film speed denotes how sensitive it is to light — the higher the ISO number then the more sensitive the film. So an ISO 100 film needs a lot of light to capture an image and it could cause problems if you are taking a picture in dimly lit conditions. A film with an ISO rating of 400 is capable of producing images when there are much lower levels of available light. The downside of the film speed equation is that the higher the film speed the grainier the final picture. This is not really an issue when using an ISO rating of 400 but it can become evident if you are using a very fast film, such as an ISO 1600.

Due to its low equivalent film speed rating it can be difficult to capture action shots, such as sporting events, with a digital camera. In general, to achieve this you need to use a very fast shutter speed (approximately 1/500th of a second or faster) and this makes it very difficult for a digital camera to get enough light onto the image sensor. Some models offer a continuous shot function whereby the camera takes several shots consecutively in the space of a second or so.

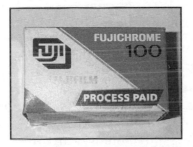

The memory chips of digital cameras are roughly equivalent to a traditional 100 ISO film. However, as the technology develops, the digital range will expand

In order to help people who are used to ISO numbers and film speeds, digital cameras provide an equivalent for their image sensor's sensitivity. This means it is the film speed it would have if it actually was a film rather than an image sensor. The most common ISO equivalent rating given for digital cameras is 100. This means that the image sensor needs the same lighting condition as an ISO 100 film to perform to its best capabilities. This is a fairly low rating and illustrates that digital cameras need plenty of light to perform to their full potential. However, the technology is improving all of the time and this rating will undoubtedly improve considerably in the coming years. Experiment taking images in different lighting conditions to see how they are handled by the image sensor.

Resolution

Although the topic of resolution was touched on in Chapter One it is a subject that can always benefit from a little revision, particularly when you are thinking about buying a digital camera.

Some digital cameras have several resolution settings, including one for capturing exactly what is seen through the viewfinder. This results in a high resolution but also large files.

Camera resolution

The camera resolution is the number of pixels that a camera is capable of capturing on the image sensor. The headline figure quoted by camera manufacturers will be as a total (1.3 million) or as the pixel dimensions (1280 x 960). Most cameras have at least two settings, so you can have a low resolution (640 x 480) if you only want to display an image on a computer monitor or email it to a friend, or a higher resolution (1280 x 960) for printing images.

Camera compression

In order to reduce file size, digital cameras can compress images by discarding unnecessary or redundant pixels. This creates smaller files and also results in images with a lower resolution.

Since all digital cameras deal with compression differently it is not possible to give a definitive guide to how this will affect separate systems. One way to judge the compression of comparable cameras is to see how many images they can store on the same memory card at the maximum compression setting. If one model can store more images it means that it creates smaller file sizes but the resolution is not as high.

The size of a file is set by the number of pixels in it. If it is compressed then it has less pixels in it and is subsequently smaller.

Resolution, compression and file size

How you use the resolution and compression settings on your camera will determine not only the quality of your images but also the size of the files that you create. For instance, on low compression and high resolution an image could take up 1.5 Mb, while on high compression and low resolution the same image may only be 500 Kb, or less. Before you start taking pictures it is worth determining what the final image is going to be used for so that you can set your resolution and compression accordingly.

Memory

On-board memory is rapidly going out of fashion and removable memory is developing so that more and more images can be fitted onto a single card.

Memory for storing digital images within a camera comes in two main types:

- On-board memory. This is similar to the memory capacity of a computer's hard drive (although much smaller). The images are stored within the camera and once the memory is full you cannot take any more images until you delete some from the memory or download them to your computer

- Removable memory. This comes in the form of the discs mentioned in Chapter Two (floppy, CompactFlash, SmartMedia and PC Card) and varies in price according to the size. Apart from floppy discs, removable memory can usually be bought in sizes ranging from 4 Mb to 192 Mb

As a general guide, an 8 Mb card can hold around a dozen images at the highest resolution and lowest compression, and 80 images at the lowest resolution and highest compression.

Once a removable memory card is full it can be replaced by a new one and you can continue shooting.

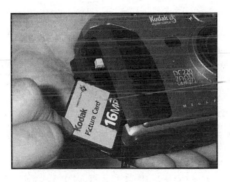

Memory cards are usually inserted into a slot in the side of the camera

It is useful to have a camera that tells you how many images you can capture on your memory card or on-board memory. This should change if you change the resolution or compression settings.

The type and amount of memory that you have with your camera is largely dependant on how you intend to use it:

- If you are only going to be taking a few snapshots and will never be far from a computer, then a 4 Mb card or even a floppy disc would be sufficient

- If you are going to be capturing a lot of images in a setting away from your computer (wildlife or travel photography for instance) then you will need a lot of cards with as much memory as possible on them

LCD panel

Once the novelty of using an LCD panel has worn off (and this may be when you have drained your first set of batteries) create your own guidelines for its use. Try not to use it to review every image that you take, but run through a whole set when you have finished. If possible, program the relevant settings into your camera through your computer before you start shooting. This way you will not have to keep changing the settings via the LCD panel.

A large number of digital cameras come fitted with LCD panels and it is an innovation which has considerable advantages, but also a few drawbacks. However, the advantages greatly outweigh the disadvantages and this will undoubtedly become a standard feature on all digital cameras in the near future.

The LCD panel is a small screen at the back of the camera that can be used to review images that have been captured in the camera and change the settings within the camera. This can be very useful for the following reasons:

- You can review pictures that you have just taken and decide whether you want to keep them or not

- You can edit the images in the camera and delete any you do not want, thus freeing up more memory. This is useful if your memory card is full and there are still some shots that you want to capture

- Through dialog menus you can change the resolution, compression, exposure and lighting settings and also add basic effects to your images such as borders. In many ways this replaces the setting controls on a conventional camera

The drawbacks to a LCD panel are:

- It uses up a lot of battery power. When digital camera users mention this in relation to LCD panels they are not taking about days or weeks, they are talking about minutes. If you use an LCD panel to review or edit images for much more than 20–30 minutes then you will soon find that your batteries are running down. This is especially so if you are using the LCD panel as an additional viewfinder

To save batteries, use a mains AC adapter to review and edit your images whenever possible.

- It is another piece of delicate technology that has the potential to malfunction

- There is the potential for making mistakes, such as deleting all of your images by accident

An additional viewfinder

As well as their reviewing and programming functions, LCD panels can also be used as an additional viewfinder to frame and capture images. If you turn the LCD panel on when you are in picture capture mode you will see a moving image appear in the panel, a bit like a video camera. This is the same (or nearly the same) view as you will see through the standard viewfinder and you can frame your image this way. This can be useful if you want to take close-up pictures of items in inaccessible places.

If the LCD panel is being used as a viewfinder it can sometimes be difficult to see the image if bright light is falling on the panel. In some cases you may have to move the camera slightly to see the image clearly, but this may then alter the framing of your shot.

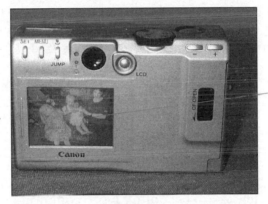

A LCD panel can be used as a viewfinder to take pictures or to review ones that have already been captured

Although using the LCD panel can be useful for specific instances it should not be used as the standard method of framing your images. This is because:

- Using the LCD panel in this way can use up the batteries at an even more alarming rate than reviewing pictures (imagine running a video camera with 4 AA batteries)

- Since the camera is being held away from the face it can be harder to hold it still and the resultant image could be blurry or out of focus. If you practise this technique then you should be able to get to a point when you can usually capture sharp images

Lenses

When you are investigating the lens of a digital camera, make sure that it is made out of optical quality glass. On some cheaper models the lenses are made out of plastic.

Fixed focus

As with a large number of compact film cameras, a lot of digital cameras are manufactured with a fixed focal length. This means that the distance from the centre of the lens to the film, or image sensor, is fixed at a certain setting. For a lot of 'point-and-press' cameras this is usually 35 mm, which is a good multi-purpose setting.

With digital cameras the actual focal length is different from the figure that is usually quoted on the box of the camera. This is because, as with aperture and shutter speed terminology, the digital camera companies thought that it was wise to stick to what people already know and so they provide an equivalent focal length figure. So a digital camera that has a 35 mm equivalent may only have an actual focal length of approximately 5mm. This is to do with the way the technology of the lens and the image sensor interact. As long as you know the equivalent focal length figure you do not need to know how it is arrived at.

If you are buying a camera with a zoom lens, make sure that it is an optical zoom rather than a digital one. An optical zoom is the genuine article, while a digital zoom only enlarges the object in the centre of the picture by making the pixels bigger. This is an operation that you could perform equally well with your image editing software.

Zoom lenses

As digital cameras are getting more sophisticated so zoom lenses are becoming more common on even the entry-level models. This enables you to view an image with a varying focal length, generally in a range between 35–120 mm. This allows you to view subjects at a magnified level without having to move too close to them. In some instances, the zoom lens function will sacrifice some picture quality but it is a useful option to have.

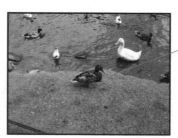

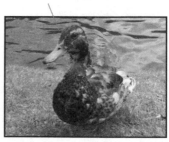

A zoom can change an average image into a striking one

Flash

The first thing to say about flashes on digital cameras is that you will not be stunned by their remarkably high power. This is one area that seems to have been left behind a little in the digital revolution, as the pressure to improve other areas has intensified. Most flashes on digital cameras in the low-to-middle end of the market are not particularly powerful and only useful for basic flash work. If you rely heavily on a flash then you will have to splash out on a higher specification model.

Although image sensors need good levels of light to operate well, some cameras take surprisingly good pictures indoors without a flash, particularly in a well lit room. Keep an eye out for the artificial light affecting the naturalness of the colours in your image though.

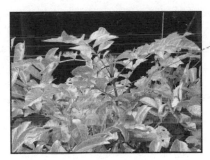

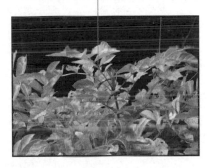

Flash can make the difference between a vibrant image and a dull one

Digital flashes often come with a number of settings:

Red-eye reduction with flashes can be a bit of a hit and miss affair. It can give the eyes a more natural look but it does not always work and it can be disconcerting for the person being photographed.

- Auto. The most straightforward flash setting on a digital camera is Auto. This means the camera decides whether there is enough light for the shot and activates the flash if conditions are too dark. This can be useful if you have misjudged the amount of available light but it can be annoying if you were not intending to use a flash

- Off. This turns off the flash completely

- On. This fires the flash with every shot, regardless of the lighting conditions

- Red-eye reduction. This fires the flash before the picture is taken and again when it is captured

Batteries

When digital cameras first appeared on the scene, battery manufacturers must have started to rub their hands in gleeful anticipation. Digital cameras use a lot of battery power. And if you are using the LCD panel you can almost see the power draining away before your eyes.

Battery usage

Battery usage has traditionally been a big problem with digital cameras. However, manufacturers have been addressing the problem and the situation is improving with most models. One of the best performers in this respect is the Mavica from Sony, which can operate for approximately an hour on one set of batteries.

The best news about batteries and digital cameras is that there is an accepted standard for the type that is used — the AA. In some cameras you can use lithium batteries, which last two or three times longer than standard alkaline batteries. Check when you are buying a camera what types of batteries it takes and how many images (roughly) they will be able to capture per set. There are also a few general guidelines that can be applied:

- Take the batteries out of the camera if it is inactive for long periods of time

- Replace sets of batteries in their entirety. Do not just replace two batteries out of a set of four

- Do not mix alkaline batteries with other types

Rechargeable batteries

Look for cameras that have a display that tells you how much life there is left in your batteries. This can save you from being caught out if your batteries pack up without warning.

Considering how quickly standard alkaline batteries can be used up by a digital camera, it is reasonable to say that rechargeable batteries are a necessity rather than an optional extra. These usually come in the form of NiCad or NiMH batteries. Some cameras come with a battery charger and rechargeable batteries and this is one of the most useful accessories you can get.

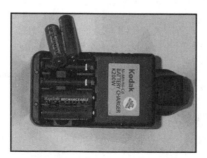

A battery charger and rechargeable batteries will more than pay for themselves in the long run. Go for NiMH batteries if possible

Additional features

TV playback

One useful feature on a digital camera is the ability to show images via a television screen. This way you can set up your own slide shows for friends and relatives without having to worry about projectors or screens.

For a television playback display you can set the camera to display the images automatically and even determine the length of time they remain on screen. In some cases you can set the playback to run continuously.

If your camera supports this function, you can set up a television playback display by selecting the relevant mode on your LCD panel and then inserting a video cable into the camera and your television. Then, when you press the relevant Start button on the camera, your images will appear on the screen.

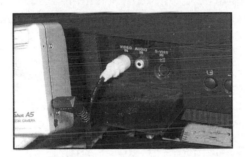

By cabling your digital camera into a television, it is possible to view your images in your living room

Image information

Different cameras have different additional features. It is best to decide first which ones you want and then try and find a camera that satisfies these needs.

Via the LCD panel it is also possible to view information about individual images, in much the same way as you would with files on a computer. The type of information that is available for each image is:

- File name. The individual name of each image

- Date and time of capture. This can also be displayed on the final image, if desired

- Aperture setting. Displays the equivalent f-stop number for each image

- Shutter speed. Displays the equivalent shutter speed for each image

- Flash details. Displays the type of flash that was used for each image

Camera software

When you link up your camera and computer, error messages can appear for a variety of reasons:

- *the camera is not connected properly*
- *the camera is not turned on*
- *you have more than one type of the system software running*

When you are assessing digital cameras it is important to keep an eye on the software with which they are supplied. This usually consists of two types: system software and imaging software.

Camera to computer communication

The software linking the camera to the computer is an integral part of the camera itself — without it you will not be able to transfer your images to a computer. It will almost certainly come on a CD and the manual will include full installation instructions. What the camera software does is allow the camera and the computer to communicate with each other. Once this channel of communication is established you will be able to do several things:

- Download your images onto your computer

- Catalogue and edit your chosen images

- Change the settings on your camera

Some cameras come with software which allows you to make adjustments to the settings, via your computer. These include:

Make sure that the system software supplied with the camera is compatible with your computer. Most cameras are designed to work on PCs or Macs, but sometimes the latter require extra connection cables.

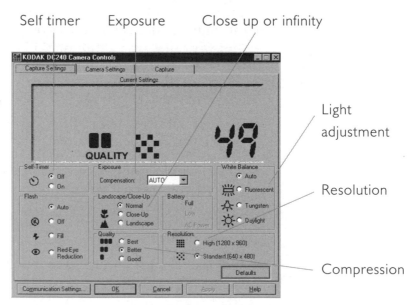

Image editing software

The type of imaging software that you get with your camera will depend on three factors:

- The camera manufacturer

- The retailer

- Your ability to haggle

The minimum you should be looking for in terms of software is a medium range editing program such as Adobe PhotoDeluxe or Ulead PhotoExpress. In some cases you may also get a cataloguing program such as ImpactAXS and a Web authoring program. Shop around to see what is on offer in different outlets.

At present, only a few cameras come with Web page authoring software. However, this is an area that is certain to expand. So look out for more of these types of programs becoming available as part of the digital camera package.

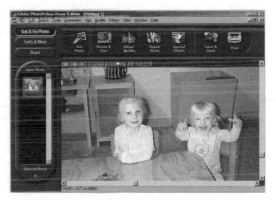

Programs such as Adobe PhotoDeluxe are sold with a lot of digital cameras and are an excellent option

It is an unfortunate fact that some retailers who sell digital cameras do not know enough about them. They either think they are a gimmick or they do not fully appreciate the entire digital process. However, if you are spending in the region of £500 on a camera then you deserve some knowledgeable service. If you are told that a camera does not come with any imaging software, or only the most basic packages, then question this. If you do not get a satisfactory response then look elsewhere. In some cases, the difference in value of the software offered can be as much as £150.

Other ways to obtain digital images

Obtaining digital images is not just a question of doing so with an expensive camera. There are a variety of other methods for getting images onto your computer:

Scanners

There is a huge variety of scanners on the market and they cover a wide range of types and prices. However, unless you are interested in investing tens of thousands of pounds on a unit that would have the power to launch a space shuttle the main options available are:

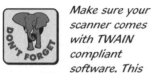

Make sure your scanner comes with TWAIN compliant software. This is a computing language that enables devices such as digital cameras and scanners to communicate with image editing programs. This means your image editing program can open your images directly from your camera, once it has been connected to the computer. Most editing software these days is TWAIN compliant.

- Flatbed scanner. This is the most common type widely available and since the costs have fallen dramatically in recent years a good quality device can be picked up for as little as £50. Most of these scanners can copy an A4 image or smaller and they operate in much the same way as a standard photocopier: the image is placed on a glass plate and then a light source is passed over it and the reflective image is captured by a Charge Coupled Device (CCD). The image can then be manipulated on a computer in the same way as one captured by a digital camera. The resolution of flatbed scanners is measured in dots per inch (dpi) and for a high quality scan you will be looking at a device with at least 600 dpi. This will cost in the region of £200 but the quality will be worth it. Having said that, the cheaper scanners also give very good results for the price

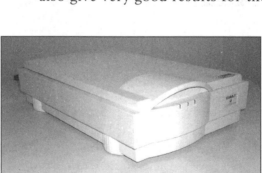

Flatbed scanners are cheap, versatile and produce excellent images

Some flatbed scanners come with adapters for scanning 35mm transparencies. These are in the form of a small box that clips onto the side of the scanner. This is a very useful addition if you have a reasonable number of transparencies that you want to digitise. Scanners with these adapters are more expensive but it could be a worthwhile investment.

- Sheet feed scanners. These are scanners that allow for an A4 sheet, or smaller to be passed through the device in much the same way as a fax machine. Although not as versatile as flatbed scanners they are a useful option if you just want to scan A4 or smaller

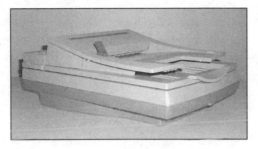

A sheet feed scanner, where the image is fed into the scanner through a paper tray

- 35mm film scanners. This could be an essential option if you have a large quantity of slide transparencies that you want to add to your digital collection. These have an adapter into which you place the transparency and which you then place into the scanner. These scanners are more expensive than flatbed ones (in the region of £400 upwards) and have a resolution from between 1200 dpi to 2750 dpi

Photo CDs

These are CDs that are capable of holding up to 650 Mb worth of digital images. These can be purchased with images already on them. The size of these images varies, up to approximately 2000 x 3000 pixels. This is good for printed output but it does produce large files that take a long time to process.

Be careful not to infringe copyright when you are downloading Web images. In theory, these have the same restrictions as hard copy images.

The World Wide Web

The Web is an excellent resource for finding images. Any image on the Web can be downloaded (select it with a right mouse click (PC) or Control+click (Mac) and then save it to your computer). There is also a variety of digital image libraries (a lot of them on the Web sites of camera companies such as Kodak and Olympus).

Future developments

The only prediction that can be made with any certainty about the future development of digital photography is that it will be rapid and far-reaching. It is still a relatively new medium, particularly for the consumer market, but the potential for growth is enormous. Some of the changes that we may see over the next few months are:

- An increased use of digital cameras as more people buy their own computers. Once someone has a computer it is a relatively small step to the world of digital photography. With prices falling constantly, household computers could eventually become as ubiquitous as the family television

- The development of the Internet raising the profile of digital cameras. As more people gain access to the Internet so they will begin to see what it can do and realise its potential. This will inevitably involve putting their own images onto the Web and so they will be looking to digital imaging. In this respect the digital camera is very much a child of the communications age

- A fall in price. One of the main drawbacks about digital cameras is their price. In order to appeal to a wider market, prices will undoubtedly fall dramatically in years to come — perhaps by as much as 50% per year

- Increased resolution. Resolution is one of the central pillars around which the medium is developed. As the technology improves this will get better and better, much in the same way as computer processing chips have evolved in the last couple of decades

- Added features. In order to capture more customers, digital camera manufacturers will include more additional features on their machines. These could include increased on-board editing functions, bigger memory cards and easier downloading options

If you dwell too much on the future developments of digital cameras you may never buy one in the present. What is bought now may be obsolete in a couple of years. You should just accept this fact gracefully and be prepared to upgrade at a later date.

The release of the latest Microsoft home operating system, Windows Me, is recognition that digital imaging is going to become an increasingly common part of the home computing revolution. It is geared towards making the downloading, storing and sorting of digital images a lot quicker and easier. For more on Windows Me, see Chapter Five.

Capturing digital images

Although some aspects of capturing an image with a digital camera are the same as with a film camera, there are some areas that are unique to the digital variety. This chapter looks at the best ways to create digital images and also some of the uses to which they can be put.

Covers

Chapter Four

Through the viewfinder

A viewfinder on a digital camera is very similar to one on a standard point-and-press camera. This means that, since it is positioned away from the lens of the camera, it views the subject from a slightly different angle. This can cause a problem known as parallax, which means that everything you see through the viewfinder will not be captured through the lens. To overcome this potential hazard, there will usually be marks around the edges of the frame which indicate the area that is going to be seen by the lens. It is important to pay attention to these marks or else it could result in parts of your image being cut off.

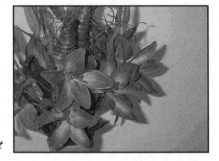

This image was correctly framed in the viewfinder but, due to parallax, it is badly positioned when captured through the lens. This problem is more pronounced with close-ups

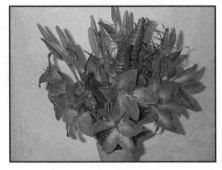

To ensure a subject is viewed correctly by the lens, it may be necessary to place it off-centre in the viewfinder

One way to get around this problem is to use the LCD panel to frame your images, since this is the same view as the one the lens sees. However, as shown in Chapter Three, there are drawbacks to this, the principal one being that it can be hard to get as sharp a picture when the camera is held at arm's length.

Focusing

Anyone who has ever fiddled with the focus controls on a manual focus camera will appreciate the advances that have been made in this area in recent years and the options that are now available. Manual focusing is available on the more sophisticated models of digital camera, but the standard ones have two main settings: fixed focus or autofocus.

Fixed focus

As the name suggests this is a focusing system that is fixed in place and cannot be altered. Everything within a certain range will be in focus and anything outwith the range will not. The settings are generally from approximately 1 metre to infinity. This is fine if you are taking general or landscape shots but not so good if you want to do a lot of close-up work.

With an autofocus camera it is possible to look the focus on a certain point and then reposition the camera to capture an image. This is done by framing the subject, activating the autofocus, and then, with the shutter button still half depressed, repositioning the camera for the shot.

Autofocus

This is an increasingly popular system whereby the camera focuses automatically on the subject in the viewfinder. It does this by using light beams to measure the distance between the lens and the subject and then selects the focus accordingly.

In order for autofocus to work the user has to give the camera a helping hand. This is done by half depressing the shutter button and then waiting until the camera focuses on the subject. Once it has done this a light will appear or the camera will beep. You then proceed by fully depressing the shutter button.

Special settings

Some cameras offer special setting such as Infinity or Close-up for occasions when you may want to capture particular types of images. This sets the camera's focus to certain levels (for instance, the close-up setting may be in the range of 0.25–0.5 metres) and also sets the appropriate levels of flash. Although this can be useful for certain types of shots it can be a bit limiting too: if your subject is just out of the range of focus then you would have to reposition yourself since the focus cannot be altered from the set levels.

Exposure

Some cameras allow for exposure compensation. This means the user can adjust the exposure by the equivalent of +2 or -2 in f-stops. This is particularly useful if your images are under- or overexposed. If your pictures are too dark then increase the number and if they are too bright, decrease it.

Although a lot of digital cameras automatically set the exposure (the combination of shutter speed and aperture settings that determines the amount of light falling on the image sensor), there are usually options to determine how this calculation is arrived at.

Spot metering

This is where the camera takes a light reading from the subject in the centre of the lens and makes the exposure setting accordingly. This can be useful if you are capturing an image against a very light background. Since the exposure is being taken from the centre of the frame it should be correctly exposed and therefore balanced with the brighter background.

Centre-weighted metering

This is similar to spot metering in that it takes the main light reading from the subject in the centre of the image. However, it also measures the light around the edges of the image too, although it still gives prominence to the centre.

Multi-pattern metering

This method arrives at an exposure reading by measuring the amount of light in the whole image, not just the centre. This is similar to putting a grid over the image and taking light readings from each individual cell. This is probably the best setting for general use, but in the above example it would result in the subject in the centre being underexposed.

When you first get a digital camera, experiment with the exposure settings. You will be able to see the results immediately and get to know the effects it produces. This will make you more confident when you are taking shots that really matter.

Experimenting with settings

The majority of digital cameras have default exposure settings which usually involve a multi-pattern reading. It is perfectly feasible to take all of your digital photographs without ever changing the exposure settings, and you will probably achieve good results. However, it is a good idea to experiment with the various exposure settings on your camera. This will give you more options when you are capturing images and it may come in useful if you are ever in a situation that requires a particular exposure setting because of the lighting conditions.

Using light

Since image sensors have an equivalent ISO rating of 100 (i.e. they need a reasonable amount of light to function effectively) it is sometimes necessary to use a little finesse when capturing images in dimly or very brightly lit circumstances.

Shooting in low light

If you are faced with capturing a digital image under poor lighting conditions there are a number of options:

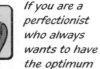

If you are a perfectionist who always wants to have the optimum lighting conditions then you could be in for a long wait on occasions. Some photographers have been know to wait for weeks to get the perfect light. At least with image editing software there is now an alternative if you do not have time on your hands.

- Come back when the light has improved

- Take the shot and hope that you can edit the image sufficiently with your image editing software

- Use flash if the subject is within range

- Try to use an additional light source

- Increase the exposure setting by one or two f-stop equivalents:

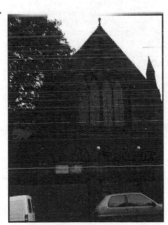

This image was captured at dusk, using the available light, and is too dark

This image was captured at the same time as the one above, but with the exposure setting at +2, and is therefore much clearer

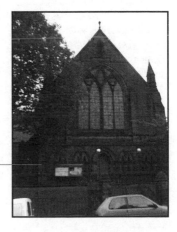

Adjusting lighting problems

Although light is usually the digital photographer's friend, there can be occasions when there is either too much light or it is coming from the wrong place. One instance of the latter is if there is one small area of light that is a lot brighter than the rest of the image. This could be sunlight reflecting on a window or a burning match. The result is that a *hot spot* appears in the final image i.e. an area where the amount of light has created a bright, white blur. It is possible to try and rectify this by adjusting the exposure but the two most effective remedies are:

- Reposition yourself so that the bright light is not in the image

- Use something to shade the offending items out of the image. This could be something as simple as holding up your hand to cover the glare from reflected sunlight

White balance is the term given to remedying indoor lighting problems. This will often be referred to in relation to Fluorescent and Tungsten controls.

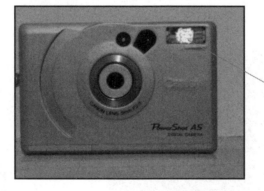

The light reflecting on the glass on this camera has created a hotspot

Another problem area with lighting can be if you are capturing images indoors without a flash. This can result in the image taking on a green or reddish-orange tint, depending on the type of indoor lighting. Some cameras let you adjust this so that your images have a more natural appearance. Look out for Fluorescent and Tungsten controls, which are the ones that correct the green or reddish-orange tints.

Fill-in flash

If you are capturing images on a bright sunny day you may think you have the ideal shooting conditions. However, there is one stumbling block that can occur under these circumstances and this is called backlighting. This happens when you are capturing an image, usually of people, when they have their back to the sun, resulting in their face and front being in shadow. The subsequent image can be unsatisfactory, as it appears to be a bright sunny day in the background and yet the subject looks dull and uninspiring.

There are a few ways to deal with backlighting:

- Ask the subject to move so that the light source is facing them

When using fill-in flash, make sure you are reasonably close to your subject. Otherwise the flash will not be powerful enough to brighten up the areas of shadow.

- Increase the exposure on your camera

- Use fill-in flash to make your subject as bright as the background.

The option of fill-in flash is probably the most effective for rectifying backlighting problems. One point to remember is that you may have to turn the flash on, rather than relying on the camera to shoot it automatically: if it is a bright day it may calculate that a flash is not required.

Photoshop Elements, the latest image editing program from Adobe, has a function for adding fill-in flash to parts of images once they have been taken and downloaded onto a computer.

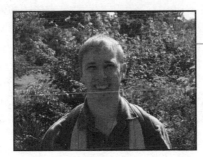

When shooting into the sun the subject's face can appear in shadow

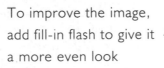

To improve the image, add fill-in flash to give it a more even look

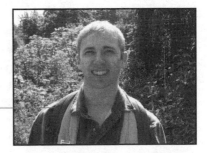

Depth of field

The depth of field in an image is the area in front of and behind the subject that remains in focus. Depth of field is an important consideration if you want to have a subject that is sharply in focus while the background is blurred:

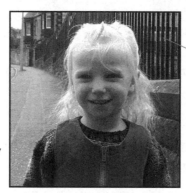

In some images a distracting background can take attention away from the main subject of the image

If you want to create an image with a blurred background and you cannot generate this through depth of field, then a similar effect can be achieved with image editing software. The main subject can be isolated from the rest of the image and then a blurring or softening effect can be added to the background.

Of course, if you can achieve this in the original image then you will save yourself some editing work...

By decreasing the depth of field the background becomes out of focus and less prominent. This can be done by using a wider aperture setting, if the camera allows

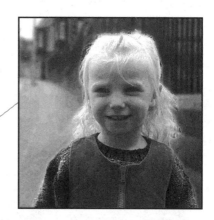

This can be an effective technique because it gives more prominence to the main subject in the image. If the image is captured with a larger depth of field then the main subject gets slightly lost in the background. This can be particularly distracting if the background is multi-coloured or it contains numerous different items.

Depth of field can be changed by moving the subject in relation to the background. A few digital cameras currently on the market offer settings that can affect the depth of field. However, most of them do not and it is a case of experimentation and improvisation. This is undoubtedly one area that will improve as digital cameras develop.

Depth of field is also affected by the type of lens being used. A telephoto lens has a much lower depth of field (less of the area will be in focus) while a wide-angle lens creates a greater depth of field.

Depth of field is altered by changing the aperture setting on a camera: the wider the aperture then the less the depth of field i.e. the area of the image that remains in focus is reduced. However, since a lot of digital cameras currently on the market do not allow for manual changes to the aperture, the best way to change the depth of field is to move your subject so that there is a greater distance between it and the background. Either that, or move yourself.

Altering the depth of field with digital cameras works best with close-up shots, when there is a reasonable distance between the subject and the background.

When you are capturing landscape shots, one consideration for depth of field is when you want to capture a foreground element in focus *and* the background features. To achieve this you may have to experiment with capturing the image from different viewpoints, unless you can move any of the elements of the image. The focal length of a lot of digital cameras allow for a large depth of field to be captured and so it is usually reasonably easy to keep the foreground and the background in focus.

If you achieve a depth-of-field effect that you particularly like, check the exposure at which the image was captured (this can usually be done through the image information control on the LCD menu). This may help you to recreate the effect in the future.

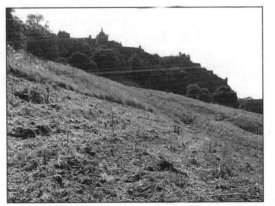

A large depth of field enables you to capture scenic images that offer both detail and perspective

Landscapes and landmarks

Capturing images of stunning scenery and notable landmarks is a popular area of photography, particularly for the holiday-maker or the travel photographer. With a digital camera the process is simplified because you do not have to carry a bulky camera and numerous rolls of film with you. Just stock up on memory cards and batteries and set off into the wide blue yonder.

Landmarks

When capturing landmarks, whether they are international, national or local, the first thing to remember is that they have probably been photographed thousands of times before. We have all seen picture-postcard shots of the Statue of Liberty or the Eiffel Tower. If you are capturing an image of a famous building or statue, bear in mind what has gone before and try and be a little bit different.

One way this type of image can be given an extra dimension is to capture it from an unusual angle. Instead of standing face on to your subject, look at it from above or below to get a new perspective. It may take a little more time than a standard shot but it will be worth the effort. Otherwise you might as well buy a postcard.

Another way to liven up a landmark shot is to have another object of interest in the picture. Sometimes this may depend on luck — if a hot air balloon floats past as you are capturing the Leaning Tower of Pisa — or else you can be creative and add your own props. This could be in the form of an object or a person. Use your imagination but do not do anything that may harm the object you are capturing. You could include items such as:

- A colourful piece of material placed in an image with subdued colours — such as a red handkerchief placed in the hand of a statue

- Items such as flowers or flags

- Other people — interesting-looking people can make great props next to landmarks

If you are travelling abroad with your digital camera, make sure you know the voltage of the power supply in the country you are visiting. Find out if you need an adapter and take one with you rather than relying on getting one when you arrive.

If you are going to be away from home and intend capturing a lot of images, consider the security of your full memory cards. Either send them back home or store them as securely as you would your passport.

Landscapes

If you are there, a glistening mountain range or a stunning sunset can be a wonderful sight. If this is then captured on a digital camera it can result in an excellent image. However, if you are displaying your holiday snaps, one shot of a beautiful sunset can be dramatic but a dozen can become tedious.

The best lighting conditions for photography are usually first thing in the morning and early evening. Always consider the quantity and quality of light when you are capturing images.

It is a fact of life that we all like to see images with people in them, even if it is people we do not know. They add perspective and meaning to an image, particularly if it involves another country or another culture.

If you are taking landscape shots try and include an object, animal or person that can act as the focus of attention in the image. This could take a number of forms:

- A climber on a mountain ridge. In instances like this, make sure that the person or object is of a sufficient size in the image to be seen properly

- A boat in front of an evening sunset. Try getting the boat silhouetted by the setting sun

- A fisherman on a deserted lake. If he or she is in the process of actually catching a fish then so much the better

If you are impatient you may get a picture but it will not be the best possible one. Be prepared to wait until a suitable object appears in your image or your subject does something out of the ordinary.

- A child playing with a ball on a beach

- A single sheep in a vast field of grass

- A car driving along a dirt track, with a plume of dust rising behind it

If you make the object the centre of attention in your image this will give it added impact and also serve to emphasis the natural beauty of the scenery. However, this does not mean that you have to position your object in the actual centre of the image. An off-centre object frequently improves the composition of an image and this is known as the rule of thirds (see page 83).

Buildings

Exteriors

Building have always been a popular choice of subject matter for photographers. If you want to go for an artistic shot then, through the use of different angles and viewpoints, buildings can be given an unusual or interesting appearance. On the other hand, if you just want a straight shot of a building (perhaps for an advertisement if you are selling a house) then this can be created quickly and easily with a digital camera.

If you cannot stand far enough back to capture the whole of a building you will have to use a wide angle lens. If you have a fixed lens then you will have no choice but to try and take the shot from a different angle.

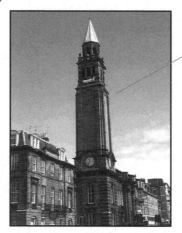

A standard view of a building provides a traditional, if somewhat predictable, image

Using a telephoto lens to capture buildings flattens the perspective and gives the building a more imposing appearance.

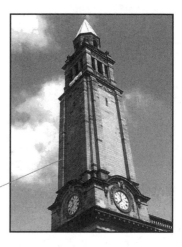

Looking at the building from a different angle gives the image a much greater impact

One of the most important factors when capturing the exteriors of buildings is perspective. This can affect a shot of a building where the straight lines of the subject seem to merge together (also known as converging parallels). This happens most frequently with tall buildings and the best way to avoid it is not to tilt the camera when you are trying to fit in the whole of a tall building. Having said that, there can be circumstances when this gives an interesting artistic effect.

Interiors

Images of buildings do not have to be restricted to exterior shots and there are a variety of uses for interior images:

- A catalogue of a house's contents for insurance purposes

- The layout of a room for the work of an interior designer

- The condition of a room for use by an insurance adjuster.

Within the interiors category there are two elements that should be considered: images of an entire room and close-ups of particular features. The former will probably require a wide-angle lens while the latter will require some form of zoom lens, if possible. Images of an entire room can be very effective but it is harder to capture a good, even image, particularly if it is a large room. In some cases one or more close-up shots will give a better impression of the room. For instance, a close-up of a stained glass window in a church may create a more eye-catching image than one of the whole interior, where large portions of the image are gloomy and nondescript.

One of the major considerations for interior photography is the amount of light. Flash units on the majority of digital cameras only operate effectively up to a distance of approximately 15 feet. This renders them ineffective if you are trying to capture a large room that has little natural light. In circumstances such as these you can either try and create an additional light source or take the shot without flash. Unless the end result is terminally gloomy you may be able to enhance the brightness of the image with your editing software.

If you want to capture interior images of public buildings, such as museums or churches, always ask permission first. In some of these places, photography is prohibited but they may give you permission if you explain what it is for.

People

Even if you are happy with a group shot once you have viewed it on the LCD panel, take a couple more to be on the safe side. It is not always possible to see all of the detail and there may be a blemish that is only visible when the image is viewed on a computer monitor.

Capturing images of people and children is one of the most popular uses for any kind of photography. However, a digital camera and its ability to review images immediately offer an added dimension — both the photographer and the subjects can see the images immediately and make any necessary adjustments accordingly.

Group shots

The greatest problem in capturing groups of people is that at least one person is always blinking or looking in the wrong direction when the picture is taken. With traditional film this does not become evident until the developing process has been completed. However, with a digital camera this can be spotted immediately, via the LCD panel, and another shot taken.

When you are photographing a group of people take a few shots and let everyone see the images on the LCD panel. They will then know how they look in the image and make any adjustments that they see fit.

You can include yourself in a group shot if your camera has a self-timer option. However, these shots frequently look a bit unnatural, as everyone is staring at the camera wondering when the shutter is going to go off. Take two or three shots like this, so that everyone can get used to the method.

Rather than having a static group of people staring at the camera it is always a good idea to arrange people in a variety of positions (standing, sitting, kneeling and even lying down) or ask them to position themselves around an additional object, such as a bench or a car. This will create an image that is more original — plus it will be more fun preparing the shot.

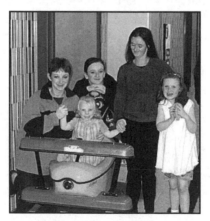

This group shot is made interesting by the composition of the people and the way they are arranged around the children's toy aeroplane

Portraits

Since a large number of digital cameras only have the equivalent of a fixed focus 35 mm lens, close up portraits are not always possible. Some models do have zoom lenses (up to about the equivalent of 120 mm focal length) and these should be considered if you want to take a lot of portraits.

If you want to take a portrait of someone, give them a reasonable amount of advanced warning. Tell them where you want to capture the image (inside or outside) and if you would like them to wear a particular item of clothing. This will give them the chance to prepare themselves and so they will feel more relaxed.

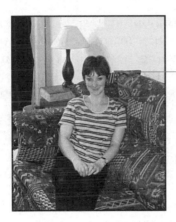

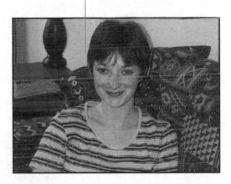

A zoom lens can make all the difference when you are capturing portraits of people. Look for a camera that has this facility

If you take a lot of sporting images and want to produce these digitally then, at present, you would be best served by a good quality SLR film camera and a scanner. This will change as the digital technology improves but this is the position at present.

If you want an action portrait of someone then your options are more limited than with conventional cameras. This is because a digital camera's recycling time is longer than that of its film counterpart. This means it takes longer for the camera to be ready from one shot to the next. With a film camera this could be less than half a second (and in some cases much less) while with the majority of digital cameras the figure is in the range of two to five seconds. This puts considerable restraints on capturing consecutive shots of people engaged in action situations. Some mid range models do have a *burst* facility which takes several pictures in succession but their present quality is such that they cannot be relied upon for genuinely fast action shots.

Children

Portraits

Children can be both a joy and a menace to capture with a digital camera. They love the immediacy of seeing themselves on a mini screen seconds after the image was taken. This can result in them wanting to become more involved in the photographic process, which can have its advantages and disadvantages.

Children love digital cameras because they can see the images immediately. However, be careful about handing them over into little hands. Not only is there the chance of sticky hands getting into places that are best left alone, there is always the possibility of the camera being dropped or bumped. Remember, this is an expensive piece of equipment.

The most common images of children, and the ones most likely to adorn the mantelpieces of parents and grandparents, are the face-on portraits with the child looking directly at the camera. With a little planning these can be made to look even more appealing than usual:

- Take the image against a neutral background. Children are invariably surrounded by the clutter of their busy lives and while this is a useful way to keep them occupied, it can detract from a staged portrait

- Move down to their level. This will make them feel more comfortable and also result in an image in which they are not staring up at the camera

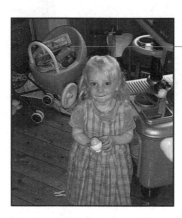

This image has a distracting background that detracts from the subject

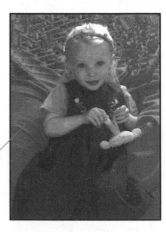

With a neutral background the subject is given more prominence

Activities

Another popular way to capture images of children is to do so when they are engaged in a particular activity. This shows them in their natural environment, when their attention is diverted away from the camera. Some areas to consider for this are:

If you are taking images of children in swimming pools, using the LCD panel to frame the image is a good way to get an effective shot without having to physically get too close to the water. This can create the impression that you too were in the water when the image was captured.

- Playgrounds

- Swimming pools

- Soft play areas

- Zoos or animal parks where the children are allowed to touch and ride on the animals.

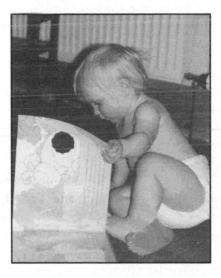

Children do not always do exactly what you expect when you are photographing them. Be patient and be prepared to take a lot of shots to get the one you want.

A good technique for capturing images of children is to do so when they are occupied or involved with an activity such as reading

Children's natural propensity for perpetual motion can sometimes cause a few problems when you are trying to capture an image with them performing a certain activity. If you are trying to catch an active child running or throwing a ball the result can be blurry and out of focus. To avoid this, try capturing these images under good lighting conditions so the shutter speed is as fast as possible and so there will be less time for the image to blur.

Business applications

Another productive use for digital images is in the business world: the price of the equipment is not such an issue as with the private user and the means for using the images is usually in place. The two main outlets for digital images in the workplace are on a Web page (a corporate Internet page or local intranet one) or in an office publication such as a magazine or a newsletter.

Capturing groups

One of the most common, and most uninspiring, office images is the one of a group of people standing in a line and staring at the camera. It may be illustrating the personnel in one division of the organisation or it may be a group of people who have won the sales people of the month award.

If you are given the job of capturing a group like this then try and liven it up a bit: rearrange them so they are not in a straight line; give them all something to hold; or ask them all to throw their arms in the air. Be innovative or else it will just be another standard, unimaginative image.

MDs and Chief Executive

Closely following the group photograph in terms of a potentially uninspiring approach is the image of the Managing Director or Chief Executive seated regally behind a desk. This may be as part of an introduction to a newsletter or on the Web home page but it is an image that has been seen thousands of times before. As above, and if you have the nerve, try and be creative with this type of image: put the MD in a different situation (in amongst the workforce for instance) or get him or her in a more relaxed pose (sitting on the edge of his or her desk perhaps). Whatever you do, get them out from behind the safety net of their desk. It will make for a better image and they may even thank you for it.

One good way to convert your MD to the idea of a more informal image is to show them the digital camera at the beginning. They may be so impressed by the technology that they will be willing to try something new themselves.

If you have to take an image of a group of people in a workplace it is a good idea to talk to them beforehand to see how they think the picture should be posed. This is a good way of generating ideas and it will put everyone in a more relaxed mood for when it comes to capturing the image itself.

If you really want to impress your MD, take a series of images of him or her and then link them together on a Web page with an authoring tool such as FrontPage.

Using business images

When you come to use your business images there are a few rules that should be followed:

- In newsletters or on Web pages use images where people are looking into the page or screen, rather than away from it off the edge. This will draw the reader's eye to the rest of the items on the page or screen

- Use images of people being active rather than sitting staring blankly at the camera:

Always tell your colleagues what you are going to use the images for. This way they do not get a surprise when they pick up a newsletter or look at the intranet and see their happy smiling faces looking back at themselves.

Some people are very reticent about having their picture displayed around the office, so a bit of sensitivity is sometimes required.

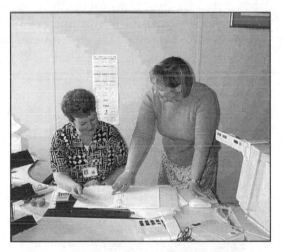

- Don't compromise on quality. If an image is not up to scratch then either reject it or take another one. A bad image can be worse than none at all

- Be careful if you are overlaying text on an image. Make sure that there is a suitable contrast between the two and that the text is not covering an important part of the picture

- If you are producing a Web site, restrict your use of images. By definition, the page will be accessed by busy people; they will be looking for business-specific information and will not want to wait a long time while a lot of images are downloaded

Composition matters

Background considerations

With film photography, some of the best shots of people can be ruined by unwanted objects in the background. These can include:

- Telephone or telegraph poles

- Object such as plants or flowers that seem to be 'growing' out of the top of the subject's head

- Other people who may inadvertently get in the shot

If you capture a shot that has an unusual or unwanted background element this can be used as a humorous image at a later date. For instance, a bridegroom who is captured with a bouquet appearing from the top of his head may see the funny side of it — but only after the traditional pictures have been delivered.

Fortunately, thanks to image editing software this is not a problem for digital photography. The images can either be removed or else the background can be softened so that they are no longer visible. However, if this problem can be avoided in the first place then it saves one extra task when it comes to the editing.

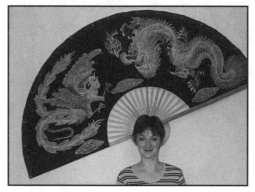

Keep an eye out for distracting background objects, although sometimes they can be used to create an unusual or humorous effect

Sometimes background elements can be deliberately incorporated into an image. This usually involves a certain amount of pre-planning or a large degree of luck. If you have a particular image in mind then try and arrange the necessary props. There was one famous image of this type when a football manager was standing in front of the club logo, which had two black triangles at either side of them. The image of the manager appeared in the press with the triangles behind him, giving him an uncanny resemblance to Batman.

Using a grid

As mentioned earlier it can improve an image to have the main subject out of the centre of the image. This can give it a more natural appearance and make it look less posed. However, it is not just a case of positioning the subject anywhere out of the centre of the image, which could result in an unbalanced picture. Imagine your image as a grid of 3 x 3 squares and position your subject at the intersection point of any of the grid lines. This should provide you with an eye-catching and balanced composition.

This is known as the *rule of thirds* and it can be applied to give an image a completely different focus. Always keep this in mind when you are capturing images and place the subject in different areas of the rule of thirds grid.

It is possible to have an image that is perfectly composed with the main subject in the middle of the shot. However, if you apply the rule of thirds it can give you a lot more flexibility when you are composing your shots.

The horizon in an image can also be composed using the rule of thirds. Try positioning it in the top or bottom third of the grid, to see what effect this has on the image.

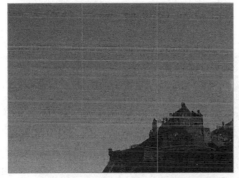

These are two images of the same subject, taken one after the other...

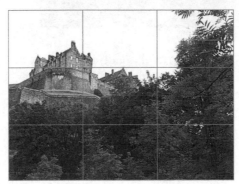

By applying the rule of thirds, two dramatically different images have been created

Composing with natural elements

When you are composing shots, the natural elements that are available can be incorporated into the final image. Some ways that this can be done are:

- Using the horizon as a natural division in your image. Moving the position of the horizon gives more prominence to different parts of the image. In some cases you may want to move the horizon to near the bottom of the image to emphasis the vastness of a subject's surroundings. On other occasions you may want to move the horizon to near the top of the image to lend greater significance to the subject of the picture

- Using natural objects to frame a subject. This is similar to putting the image in a frame once it has been captured. However, if the frame occurs naturally then this gives the image extra relevance

It is perfectly acceptable to break the rules of composition and achieve dramatic results. However, it is best to get the hang of the basics first:

- *Capture some images using the rule of thirds and utilising negative space*
- *Look at the results and see what similar scenes look like if you ignore these rules or apply the opposite*

As you do this you may even develop your own rules of composition.

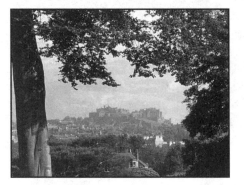

Trees and bushes are excellent for creating natural borders around a subject

- The natural space in an image. Do not underestimate the value of space in an image. It can be used to emphasis the vastness of a scene and give the subject a chance to express itself. This is often referred to as *negative space* and this should be kept in mind, particularly when capturing large objects. Do not just look at the subject of an image; give some consideration to the space around it and how this will affect the composition of the image.

Using Windows Me

The latest home edition of Microsoft's operating system, Windows Me (Millennium Edition), is designed to make working with digital images as easy as possible. This chapter shows how to get the most out of Me and harness its considerable capabilities for improving the digital imaging process.

Covers

Chapter Five

Downloading images

The minimum requirements for using Windows Me are:

- *Pentium, or equivalent, 150 MHz or higher processor*
- *32 Mb of RAM (a minimum of 64 Mb is desirable to make Me run more effectively)*
- *VGA resolution or better monitor*
- *CD-ROM or DVD-ROM drive*

To make full use of all of the features of Me it is also desirable to have items such as a 56 Kbps modem, a sound card and speakers.

Windows Me is the successor to the immensely successful Microsoft operating systems for PCs, Windows 95 and 98. The main difference with Me is that Microsoft have recognised the growing importance of digital issues for the home computer user and designed the software accordingly. In addition to increased functions for playing and editing video and music files, Me also comes with a system to greatly simplify the process of getting digital images from the camera to the computer. This is known as Windows Image Acquisition (WIA) and it helps to not only get your images onto your system, but also to add new devices such as scanners and digital cameras.

If you are currently using Windows 95 or 98 it is not essential to upgrade to Me. However, if you do a lot of work with digital images, or plan to in the future, then it is an investment that is well worth making.

Adding images with Me

If you have installed your camera or scanner software then you will be able to start downloading images with Me immediately. Before you start, make sure your digital device is turned on, connected to the computer and, for a camera, turned to the Connect setting.

Windows Me takes up between 240 Mb and 400 Mb of hard disc space when it is installed. In addition, the installation process can take up to an hour.

1 Select Start > Programs > Accessories > Scanner and Camera Wizard from the Taskbar

2 On the first page of the Scanner and Camera wizard, select Next

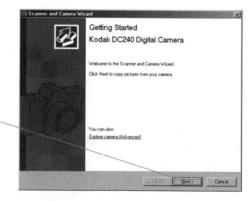

When images are downloaded, they are all numbered sequentially, regardless of the textual title that they have been given.

3 Click Select All to select all of the images for downloading. Or Ctrl+click to select specific images. Select Next

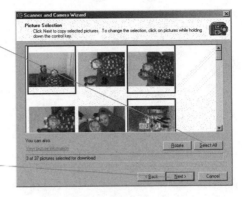

If you have a USB (Universal Serial Bus) connection for your camera or scanner you will find that it operates with impressive speed with Me. Downloading images with this method can now take seconds, rather than minutes as is the case with the older method of serial cable transfer.

4 Select a description for how you would like the images named (the default is Picture) and select a folder where you would like them saved to on your system. Select Finish

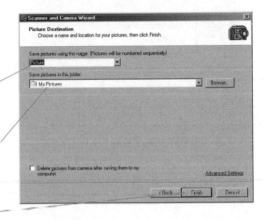

When your images have been downloaded into a sub-folder, it is a good idea to add some kind of a description to the date that Me includes. This will make it easier when you are searching for specific images in the future.

5 The images are downloaded into a new sub-folder of the location selected in Step 4. This is named with the date on which the images were downloaded

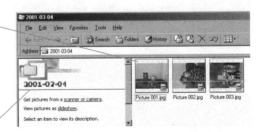

Adding digital devices

Windows Me allows you to add numerous digital devices, without also having to load separately the software to operate them. To do this:

1 Select Start>Settings>Control Panel from the Taskbar

2 If the Camera and Scanner icon is not showing, select View all Control Panel options

Windows Me has an enhanced Plug and Play facility, that allows you to install and use new hardware, such as a digital camera or a scanner, without having to restart your system once the software for the device has been added.

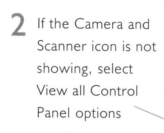

3 Double-click on the Scanners and Cameras icon

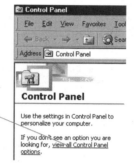

Windows Me contains drivers (the software that lets a digital device communicate with the computer) for the most common digital devices. This means that it can install the software without the need for a disc. However, you may still need a disc if you want to use additional software that comes with the device.

4 Double-click on the Add Device icon

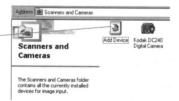

5 Complete the Installation Wizard for the device you want to add to your computer. Select Next on each page

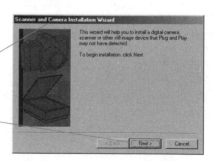

Viewing images

One of the great benefits of Me is that you can view your images without having to first open them in a separate image editing program. This can save a lot of time, since you can use Me to identify the images you want to use and then use an image editing program to work with these specific images. If you do not want to edit the images you can then use Me to print or email the required items. To view images with Me:

Windows Me only has very basic image editing functions, such as rotating the view of an image. Image editing programs and their functions are looked at in Chapters Six and Seven.

1 Using Windows Explorer, open a folder containing digital images

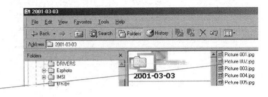

The Thumbnails view can also be accessed by selecting View> Thumbnails from the toolbar.

2 Click here and select Thumbnails, to view reduced versions of the images

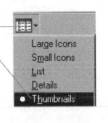

3 Select an image. A larger version will be displayed in this preview box

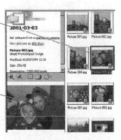

Click here to get a full size preview of a selected image.

4 Click on the magnifying glass icons and then click on the image in the preview box to zoom in or out

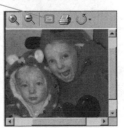

Basic functions

Although Me does not have the functions of a dedicated image editing program, it is possible to perform some very basic operations.

Naming images

If you double-click on an image name to try and rename it, this will open it in your default image editing program.

1 Click once on the name of an image. Wait a couple of second, then click once on it again. The name should be highlighted

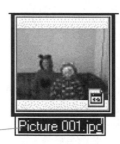

When renaming images, make sure that you include the file extension i.e. 'JPG'. If you don't, the system may not be able to recognise the file type of the image and so it will not be able to open it.

2 Insert the new name by overtyping. Press Enter or Return

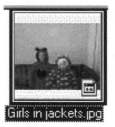

Rotating

Click here to rotate an image clockwise (right) or counter clockwise (left)

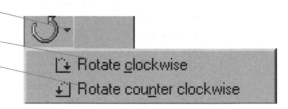

For more information on printing images, see Chapter 10.

Printing

Click here to send an image to your printer

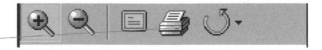

Editing and sharing

Using an image editing program
If you want to use more advanced image editing techniques, it is possible to open an image directly from Me into a dedicated image editing program. To do this:

If you are serious about using digital images you will very quickly realise that an image editing program is essential. Me's strong points are downloading and storing, rather than editing.

1 Right-click an image you want to edit. Select Open With and the image editing program you want to use

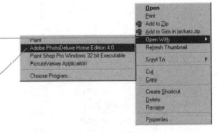

2 The image will be opened in the specified application, ready for editing

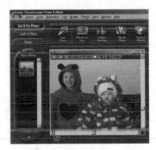

Emailing images
Me makes it easy to send images to friends and relatives, using email:

If you have a different default email program from Outlook Express, this will appear on the Send To menu. Select this program to open it and then add the recipient's name to a new message.

1 Right-click an image you want to email. Select Send To>Mail Recipient

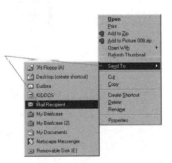

2 By default, Me opens Outlook Express, with the image attached to a message. Add the required recipient, then select Send

Slideshows

With Me the concept of family slideshows, complete with projector and screen, can become a distant memory. Instead, all of your digital images can be displayed sequentially on your computer. To do this:

1 Open the folder of images that you want to view

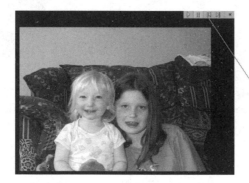

The Adobe image editing program, PhotoDeluxe, has a function for creating a more graphical slideshow, called a PhotoParade. For more information on this, see Chapter Eight, page 140.

2 Select View pictures as slideshow

3 The images are then displayed automatically in sequence. Each image is visible for approximately 10 seconds

4 Move the cursor over an image and the control bar will appear. This can be used to move through the images, pause the slideshow or stop it

Image editing software

This chapter gives an introduction to the different types of image editing software on the market. It shows how the software operates and illustrates some of the effects that can be achieved.

Covers

Chapter Six

Entry-level programs

User interface

As the popularity of creating digital images via digital cameras and scanners increases, so too does the amount of image editing software. The majority of this is aimed at the general consumer market. For approximately £35–£50 you should be able to buy a very solid editing package that will allow you to undertake a variety of editing functions and also apply some interesting special effects and touch-up techniques.

Entry-level editing packages are user friendly and the interface consists of easy to follow icons, toolbars and Help text boxes. Most also have their own library of images which are useful for experimentation before you start creating your own.

When you start working with an image editing package, set up a directory, and sub-directories if necessary, for your images. This way you will always know where to go to find your images and you will not have to jump between different directories.

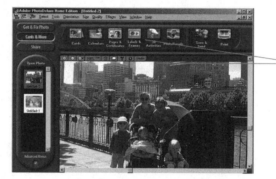

Entry-level editing packages have easy to follow graphical icons and toolbars

All editing programs work best with the monitor set for the maximum number of colours that it can view (usually 16 million). Some programs will not function unless this setting is applied.

The main functions that will be available in the editing programs are:

- Colour editing

- Applying touch-up techniques

- Creating special projects, from greeting cards to wine labels

- Emailing, or faxing, images around the world. Most programs can do this by connecting directly with your email program or fax machine

The programs

There are dozens of entry-level editing programs on the market but four of the best are:

- Adobe PhotoDeluxe. A general level program by the makers of the best-selling professional package Adobe Photoshop. It offers a Home and a Business version and it is an excellent product in terms of functions and ease of use. For more information, see the Adobe Web site at www.adobe.com

- Ulead Photo Express. Similar to PhotoDeluxe, with easy to use icons and a good range of functions but more limited project options (for more information, see the Ulead Web site at www.ulead.com):

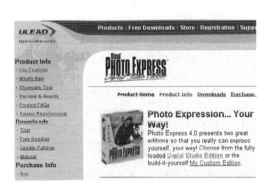

- MGI PhotoSuite. Another program in the PhotoDeluxe/PhotoExpress mode but with perhaps not such a wide range of functions. However, functionality can be in the eye of the user. For more information, see the MGI site at www.mgisoft.com

- Corel Print House. Corel is one of the market leaders in graphics and imaging programs. This is a very versatile package with a slightly different user interface from the previous three programs. Each technique is shown with a before-and-after icon so you can see immediately the type of effect to be applied. For more information, see the Corel Web site at www.corel.com

Professional programs

Price and power

If you are prepared to pay up to £500 for an image editing program then you will get a product that should fulfil all of your imaging needs and more besides.

The professional models are designed specifically for designers, graphic artists and desktop publishing specialists. They are unsurpassed in terms of colour editing functions and if this is what you are interested in then one of these programs should be considered.

The main drawback with these programs is that they can seem complicated and difficult to learn. Some prior knowledge of image editing is useful, otherwise it may take intensive use before you feel comfortable with the software.

User interface

Unlike the general level programs, the professional versions offer very little in the way of guidance for the users. The functions are contained within various toolboxes and menu bars and it is a case of trying each one to see what it does. When you are doing this, use a test image so that if you do something you are unable to correct you will not have wasted a valuable image of your own.

Professional packages have numerous menus and toolbars:

Editing tools

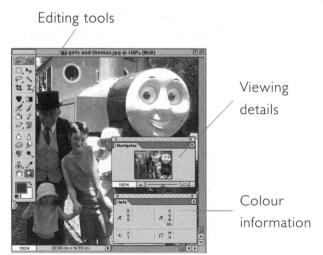

Viewing details

Colour information

The programs

- Adobe Photoshop 6. This is the top-selling image editing program and for power and versatility is it hard to beat. It can edit colours with great precision and has over 80 filters for adding special effects such as blurring and watercolour techniques. An excellent program for business users, or those who are into digital imaging in a big way. For more information, see the Adobe Web site at www.adobe.com

- Paint Shop Pro 7. For value for money this is one of the best programs on the market. The full version costs approximately £80 but a shareware version can be downloaded from the Web and this is perfectly adequate for the majority of purposes. The interface is similar to that of Photoshop but there is not the same range of sophistication. Nevertheless, it is an excellent product, which goes some way to bridging the gap between entry-level and professional programs. For more information, see the Web site at www.jasc.com:

The main drawback of Photoshop is the price, which is around £500. If this is outside your budget then Photoshop Elements (see the final paragraph on this page) may be a more realistic alternative as it costs approximately £90.

If you want to unravel the mysteries of Photoshop or Paint Shop Pro then an excellent place to start is Computer Step's own titles:

- 'Photoshop 6 in easy steps'
- 'Paint Shop Pro 7 in easy steps'

Try and use your editing programs as often as possible. This will ensure that you become completely comfortable with the software and enable you to discover new functions and techniques.

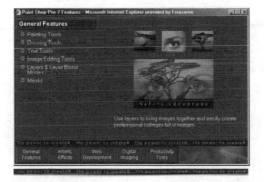

Paint Shop Pro is reasonably priced and an excellent all round editing program

- Corel PHOTO-PAINT. This is more of an image and graphics package combined. For more information, see the Web site at www.corel.com

- Photoshop Elements. This is the latest program from Adobe and it offers extensive techniques for editing and enhancing images for both print and Web publication

Opening images

Image editing software is the magic dust that transforms images by changing their basic elements (such as colour definition, brightness, contrast and saturation); enables editing techniques which can alter or remove objects in the image; and adds additional elements to the image.

If you have never seen an image editing package before then the collection of buttons and icons can be a bit overwhelming at first. But, thankfully, most of the programs work on the same principles — you obtain an image from a selection of possible sources, you make your editing changes and then you print the image, email it or publish it on the Web.

Obtaining images

When you first open an editing program you will want to open an image so that you can work on it. On the higher level programs you will just have the standard File>Open option. But with the entry-level programs you may encounter a screen that is similar to this (this is Adobe PhotoDeluxe 4 Home Edition):

If you want to acquire an image from a digital source, make sure it is connected and turned on before you try and access it. If it is not connected you will probably have to turn off your computer, connect the device and then reboot.

1 Click here to access the toolbar

2 Select an image from the computer

3 Or select an image from an imaging device or the Web

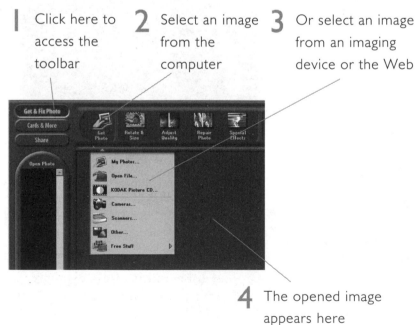

4 The opened image appears here

Opening images from the computer

When you elect to open an image from the computer the options that you are given include:

- Open an image from an image library that has already been created

- Open an image that is pre-installed with the software.

- Open a Clip Art file. It is impossible to escape from the ubiquitous Clip Art. This can be useful if you want to create a humorous montage using a photographic image and Clip Art

- Open a file from your own hard drive on the computer. To do this you will have to have already created and saved some images

Opening images from a digital device

If you want to open an image from a digital source such as a camera or a scanner you select the appropriate icon and a pick list similar to this will appear:

If you are trying to acquire an image from a digital device and it does not appear on a pick list then this is probably caused by one of two things:

- Firstly, the device is not connected properly or turned on

- Secondly, the system software connecting the device and the computer has not been installed correctly

Windows Me is designed to make the process for downloading digital images as painless as possible. For more information on Windows Me, see Chapter Five.

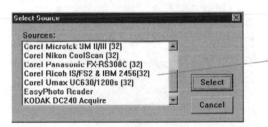

A list of suggested digital devices from which images can be obtained will be shown

There are usually a lot of irrelevant options that are included, most connected to the software in use. So scroll down until you find your digital camera or scanner listed.

If your software does not have a pick list option then there will be a dialog box into which the name of the device you want to use can be typed.

Viewing images

Once you have your image on-screen, and you have congratulated yourself on getting all of the connections and settings correct, you can then decide how you want to view it. This will depend largely on what you want to do with it:

A view of 100% or 1:1 may not occupy the whole screen in some editing packages. This will depend on the size of the actual image rather than the viewing ratio. If you want to view an image on the entire screen then select the Fit to Window command, if there is one.

- For overall colour editing, a Fit in Window setting is best. This means that all of the image can be seen on screen

- For editing that involves removing unwanted items, such as people or objects, a zoomed-in ratio of 2:1 or 3:1 is sufficient

- For very close-up work, that could require individual pixels being edited, a magnification of 10:1 or above may be required

Each program deals with magnification in a slightly different way, so experiment to see which setting suits your needs best.

If an image is viewed at a very high magnification it becomes pixelated. This means you can edited individual pixels, which can be useful for techniques such as reducing red-eye.

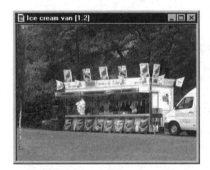

An image at 1:2 scale

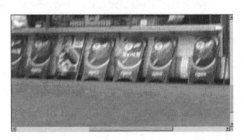

The same image at 3:1 scale

Magnification options

Each program has its own way of providing magnification controls. Some examples are:

- PhotoDeluxe has magnifying glass controls:

If you are using a magnifying glass icon to enlarge one particular area in an image you will have to reposition it for each level of magnification. This is because the point that you want to see will move its co-ordinates in the image each time.

This increases magnification for the whole image

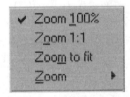

This decreases the magnification for the whole image

This increases magnification, centred on the point where the icon is placed

- Corel Print House has Zoom settings:

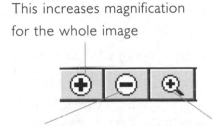

- Paint Shop Pro 7 shows the image magnification in cumulative factors:

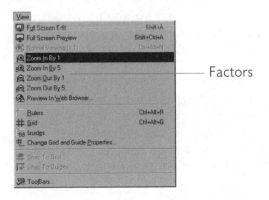

Factors

File formats

Digital images can be created and saved in a variety of different formats. This is not always immediately apparent when you view the images on screen, but the file format can have important implications as far as the use of the image is concerned.

The two main areas that designers of image file formats consider are:

GIF comes in two varieties, 87a and 89a. These are more commonly known as nontransparent GIFs and transparent GIFs respectively. With a transparent GIF the background can be made see-through. This is very useful for Web images: if you want the subject of an image to appear against the Web page background, you can do this with a transparent GIF.

- The size of files — how to get good quality images that do not take up a lot of disc space.

- The quality of images — how to produce images that give the best printed quality possible.

Because of this, different file formats are better suited for some purposes than others.

GIF files

GIF (Graphical Interchange Format) is one of the two main file formats that is used for images on the Web (the other being JPEG). It was designed with this specifically in mind and its main advantage is that it creates image files that are relatively small. It achieves this principally by compressing the image by removing unnecessary or irrelevant data in the file.

There are two methods for compressing digital images; lossy and lossless. Lossy means that some image quality is sacrificed, while the lossless method only discards image information that is not needed.

The main drawback with GIF files for digital images is that they can only display a maximum of 256 colours. This is considerably less than the 16 million colours that can be used in a full colour image. Therefore photographs in a GIF format may lose some colour definition and they will not have the same range of colour subtleties as a format that can display the full range of colours.

Despite its narrow colour range GIF is still a very useful and popular format. It is excellent for displaying graphics and even photographs can be of a perfectly acceptable standard for display on the Web. Add to this the fact that it can create very small image files and it is easy to see why GIF is so popular with Web designers.

JPEG files

JPEG (Joint Photographic Expert Group) is the other main file format for Web images and it is the one that, as the name suggests, specialises in photographic images. A lot of digital cameras automatically save images as JPEGs.

JPEG images only achieve their full effect on the Web if the user's monitor is set to 16 million colours (also know as 24 bit). Most modern monitors are capable of doing this but, in some cases, the user may have set the monitor to a lower specification. If you are concerned about how your images are going to viewed it may be worth putting a note on your site suggesting that the screen be set to 16 million colours for full effect.

As with GIF, JPEG compresses the image so that the file size is smaller; it is therefore quicker to download on the Web. One downside to this is that the file is compressed each time it is opened and saved, so the image quality deteriorates correspondingly. When a file is opened it is automatically decompressed but if this is done numerous times then it can result in an inferior image.

The main advantage of JPEG files is that they can display over 16 million colours. This makes them ideal for displaying photographic images. The colour quality of the image is retained and the file size is still suitably small.

PNG files

The PNG (Portable Network Group) file format is a relatively new one in the Web image display market but it has the potential to become at least as popular as GIF and JPEG. It uses 16 million colours and lossless compression, as opposed to JPEG which uses lossy compression. The result is better image quality but a slightly larger file size. Since PNG is a developing format there are a few factors to bear in mind when using it:

- Not all browsers support the PNG format. This will undoubtedly change as its use becomes more widespread but it is a consideration at the moment

You should note the following file extensions (the last is the least common):

GIF files — .GIF

JPEG files — .JPEG

PNG files — .PNG

- PCs and Macs use different PNG file types and, although both types can be opened and viewed on both platforms, they appear to their best effect on the platforms on which they were created

- PNG files can contain meta-tags — indexing information that can be read by Web search engines when someone is looking for your Web site

TIFF files

The TIFF (Tagged Image File Format) format is one of the most popular and versatile currently in use. It creates files that have very good image quality and it uses a lossless compression system known as LZW (Lempel-Ziv-Welsh). This is the same system as used by GIF images and it can compress files by between 50–90%, while still retaining the image quality. However, with TIFFs this leads to file sizes that are generally larger than GIFs or JPEGs, so they are used for files that are going to be printed rather than displayed on the Web.

Kodak have developed a file format that is specifically for use with images on CDs. It is called Photo CD and can store images on a CD at five different sizes. Most image editing programs can open Photo CD files but they cannot save to this format.

When a file is saved to the TIFF format a dialog box will appear that allows you to specify whether you want to apply LZW compression or not. Unless you have a good reason not to, you should select this option.

For your interest, you should take note of the following file extensions:

TIFF files — .TIF

BMP files — .BMP

EPS files — .EPS

FlashPix files — .FPX

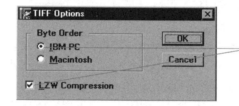

When saving a TIFF file you can determine which platform it is for and whether you want to apply compression

Other file formats

Some other file formats you may come across when you are dealing with digital images are:

There are other file formats for images but the ones discussed here are the most common.

- BMP. This stands for BitMap Part and is a Windows format that has been popular in the past; however, it is generally now only used for specialist purposes

- FlashPix. This is a new file format that has been developed by a number of photographic and computer companies. The general aim of this format is to allow higher speed editing of large image files

- EPS. This stands for Encapsulated PostScript and is usually only used when files are being prepared for commercial printers

Saving files

Most image editing packages have their own file formats (known as *proprietary formats*, see left) which they will automatically save files in, unless told otherwise. For instance, Adobe PhotoDeluxe uses its own format with *.PDD* or *.PBD* extensions and Ulead has its own format with .TPX or .UPX. The main reason to use the program file format is that it will generally speed up the editing process and it will allow any elements that are specific to that program to be applied to the image. However, if you want to then open the image in another program or place it on the Web you should select Save As and chose one of the commonly used formats such as GIF, JPEG or TIFF.

File formats that are unique to a specific program are known as proprietary formats. If you are working with these, then it is best to save a copy of the file into a more common format when you have finished editing. This way you can then open the file in another program if you want.

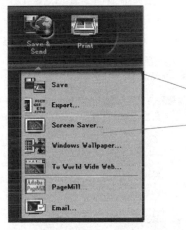

In PhotoDeluxe, the Save and Send dialog box shows the various options

Entry-level editing packages usually offer an icon-based interface, like the one above, for saving files. The professional packages will just have the standard Save and Save As commands and you then choose the file format and directory that you want.

It is possible to save files in numerous different formats. If you wanted to send a file to a printing bureau then you might save it as an EPS file, whereas if you were publishing something on the Web you could choose a JPEG format.

Touch-up techniques

Touch-up techniques go by a variety of names in entry-level programs but they all do the same general tasks — allowing the user to carry out operations like:

The top of the range image editing packages do not have such an easy to use interface for editing controls as the entry-level ones. There is the same range, or more, but this is found within the standard toolboxes and menu bars.

- Amending colour appearance

- Amending image sharpness

- Changing image orientation

- Removing unwanted elements

- Converting the image into another format, such as black and white or watercolour

A standard touch-up toolbar may look something like this one from PhotoDeluxe 4 Home Edition.

Always make a copy of an image before you start changing the size, colour or appearance. Therefore, if the editing does not turn out as expected you still have the original to fall back on.

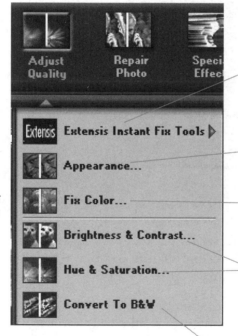

An all-in-one editing command for the whole image

Remove unwanted elements from an image

Use preset options to fix the colour

Brightness, contrast and saturation commands

Images can be changed into black and white or sepia-tinted

Special effects

As well as the standard editing techniques, image editing programs also offer a range of options that can best be described as special effects. Here is a selection:

- Distortion

- Textured

- Re-colouring

- Edge Effects

- Collages

As with the touch-up techniques, these are presented by a simple graphical interface, like this one from PhotoDeluxe:

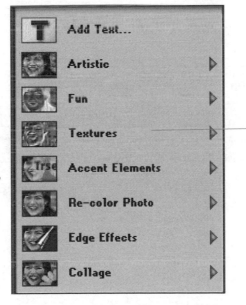

Most image editing programs have a range of special effects, similar to these ones

Some programs have dozens of these effects, while others only have a few. They are fun to use for a while, but for some of the effects the novelty wears off quite quickly.

Types of projects

Business projects

Most entry-level editing programs allow for images to be incorporated into specialist projects. From a business viewpoint this can be very useful. Everyday documentation can be given a stylish look with the introduction of a personal photograph or an image of the company's latest product. PhotoDeluxe Business Edition allows images to be included in the following:

Labels   Envelopes   Compliment slips

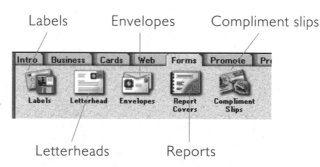

Letterheads   Reports

Personal projects

One of the really fun aspects of image editing software is its ability to include images in a variety of fun, family-orientated projects. By following the on-screen instructions, your favourite images can be transferred to any of the following:

- Calendars

- Greetings cards

- Invitations

- Screen savers

- T-shirts

- Mugs

Always check to see which programs support the projects in which you are interested.

Editing digital images

This chapter gives some editing tips and introduces some basic techniques for editing images, from colour adjustment to creating the impression of speed.

Covers

Chapter Seven

The editing process

The ability of editing software to enhance digital images should not be seen as an excuse to take sub-standard pictures in the first place. Always try and take the best shot you can — a good original image will usually be preferable to a poor image that is then digitally enhanced.

Although digital image processing is not yet at the level of a James Bond film, where a blurry dot on the horizon can be transformed into a crystal-clear image of a secret rocket launch pad, it can nonetheless achieve some dramatic effects on even the most humble snapshot. In addition to improving and tweaking the colour of images, editing packages can also change the appearance of items, get rid of the demonic-looking red-eye and even remove unwanted objects in a picture.

When you are editing digital images you should consider two main areas:

- The overall look of the images, which is controlled by various colour enhancing options

- The editing and special effects that can be applied to the whole image or to selected parts of it

The overall look of an image is concerned with whether it is too dark, too light or if the colours look pale and washed-out. All of these areas can be improved with a few straightforward editing operations. For instance, if an image is too dark then it can be lightened with the Brightness command in image editing programs. This will lighten the image and a preview option will let you view the changes as they are made.

Think of a digital image as a collection of coloured dots rather than one complete picture. It is possible to edit each of the dots, either collectively or individually, or any variation in between.

Special effect techniques enable you to add a variety of effects to an image and remove blemishes such as red-eye or scratches. This can produce dramatic results but you should be aware of the following points:

- Do not expect your images to be transformed beyond all recognition — the software can only work with what it is given

- Do not worry if your first attempts are not perfect. Persevere and you will improve

- Be as creative as you like — as long as you have saved a copy you can always go back to the start

Before you start

Editing digital images can be an extremely fulfilling task. Mediocre photographs can be transformed into images that you would be proud to show your friends and family and even use in items such as Web pages or newsletters. However, before you start sampling the delights of digital image editing software there are a few basics that should be followed:

- Digital images can be opened just like any other file on your computer. In most programs it is a case of selecting File>Open and then selecting the relevant file. Alternatively you can open an image using the Open icon on the toolbar

- Before you start editing any digital image, make a copy of it first. This way, if it all goes horribly wrong, then you can still go back to the original and start again

- Save your image frequently while you are editing it. Even though this should be done for all types of computer files it is particularly pertinent when you are editing digital images. The reason for this is that image files tend to be large and can cause computers to crash if they feel they are being asked to do too much processing. If this happens when you have undertaken a significant amount of editing then all of your work will have been lost since the last time you saved it. As a rule, save your image after every two or three edits. If this seems a little excessive, imagine how annoying it would be to have to go back to the beginning of your editing session and start again

- If you intend printing out your images then do this in draft at different stages of the editing process. Printed colours do not always look the same as on screen. If you check the printed colours as you go along then you will not be in for a nasty surprise at the end. Remember: images on photographic paper display colour to a higher quality than normal paper

Basic colour adjustment

Most people who take photographs like to see the fruits of their labours in glorious colour. The ability to produce images with striking and vibrant colours is a valuable one, but even if you take pictures where the colour is less than perfect, image editing software allows you the chance to redeem yourself.

Some editing programs have an Auto Levels command that adjusts all colour aspects of an image in a single function. Although this can be quick and effective it is generally better to adjust each colour element independently.

All imaging software has the tools to increase or decrease the main areas of colour, such as brightness, contrast and saturation. This generally changes all of the selected colour levels for the entire image. While this can produce effective results, there may be occasions when you need to lighten one area more than another, or increase the contrast on only one part of the picture. This can be done by selecting the area that you want to edit and applying the relevant colour controls to that section. So if you have a striking image and a nondescript, washed-out sky, you can select the sky area and enhance it using your colour controls.

Fans of black and white images are also provided for in image editing software and there are a number of techniques available.

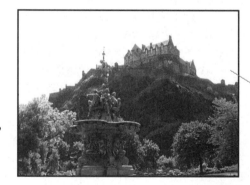

Editing software can be used to make significant changes to parts of an image

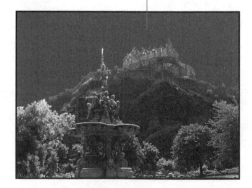

Improving brightness

When you are increasing or decreasing the brightness, work with moderate changes at a time. It is better to work gradually towards the effect you want so that you can view the variations in between. This not only lets you see how varying changes in brightness affect your image; it also enables you to become more familiar with how your editing software works.

The brightness of an image needs to be adjusted when the original picture is underexposed (dull all over) or overexposed (too much glare). This can be done by selecting the Brightness effect from your toolbox or menu bar and then applying it to the image. There will probably be a type of sliding scale, where you can define the amount you want the brightness increased or decreased.

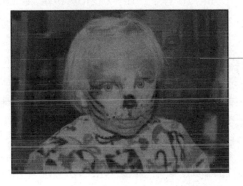

An image that is too dark would be worthless if it was from a film camera

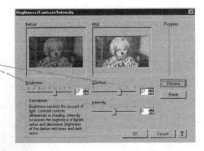

2 Select the colour controls to edit the image

Most editing software has a Preview function when you are editing an item. This allows you to see the effect before you apply it to the image.

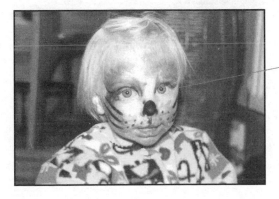

3 The final result is much more acceptable

Contrast and saturation

Contrast

The contrast in an image is the relationship between the dark and light areas in a photograph, or the tones. If the contrast is too great then the colours will look like they do not blend together properly, and if it is not enough they will not stand out sufficiently against each other. Contrast can be edited in the same way as brightness and in some programs it appears in the same dialog box. It can be beneficial to experiment with changing the brightness and the contrast together to see what effect this has on the image.

Hue can also be adjusted in the same dialog box as saturation. This alters the colour of individual pixels and can produce some interesting, surreal effects.

Saturation/Intensity

Saturation increases or decreases the intensity of colour in your image. In most editing packages this is done by dragging a sliding scale to add or remove colour from your image. This can have a dramatic effect on images that appear slightly faded or washed-out. However, be careful not to overdo it or you may end up with images that look unnaturally bright.

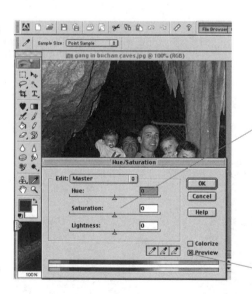

The colour saturation, hue and intensity in an image can be adjusted using sliding scales

If available, use Preview to make sure the colour changes are producing the desired effect

Correcting the balance

The colour balance is the relationship between the colours in your image. If the colours are well balanced then you should have a picture with a natural appearance, where no one colour appears to dominate. However, it is a peculiarity of digital images that they sometimes suffer from an error in colour balance. This could result in a beach scene having a blue tinge all over, indicating that the balance is incorrect and there is too much blue in the image.

In most editing software programs, the colour balance is altered either by:

- adjusting a sliding scale

or

- entering values into colour levels option boxes

On the sliding scale you can adjust the levels of three combinations: Red/Cyan, Green/Magenta and Blue/Yellow. In each case the two colours are at the opposite sides of a standard colour wheel.

There are two terms that apply to colour balance: subtractive and additive.

Subtractive involves increasing the levels of colours other than the one you want to reduce (so if there is too much blue then you increase the levels of red and green). The additive method, however, involves adding the colour at the opposite side of the colour wheel to the one you want to reduce (so to reduce the blue again, you increase the amount of yellow).

(Of the two methods, the subtractive one usually works best.)

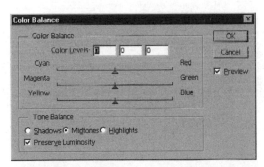

Professional programs such as Photoshop adjust the balance with sliding scales and option boxes

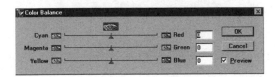

General level programs have a simpler set of sliding scales

Adjusting colours with levels

In more sophisticated editing programs, such as Adobe Photoshop, colours can be edited using a function called Levels. At first sight the Levels option is one that looks more like something from a scientific experiment than a device that is going to transform your humble images. However, if you persevere with it then the results are more satisfying than the all-in-one editors.

Do not expect to get the hang of the Levels command in a matter of minutes. It is vital that you make a copy of an image before you start applying this technique because you may well want to go back to the original.

The main difference between Levels editing and all-in-one editing is that Levels allows you to change the settings independently for different areas (highlights, shadows and midtones) of the picture. Values for each element can either be added into option boxes or they can be altered using a sliding scale. This is a fairly technical way of editing your images and one that needs a fair degree of practise.

Levels controls can be altered by adding figures into the option boxes

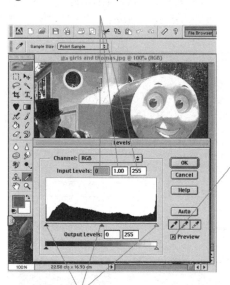

Select Preview to view the changes as you are making them

Levels can also be adjusted by moving the sliding scales. This alters the colour levels of the Shadows, Midtones and Highlights. Experiment to see how this affects different areas of your image

Selecting an area

For many editing functions it is necessary to select a specific part of an image. This allows for different techniques to be applied to separate areas of the picture. Therefore, tools to select parts of an image are a fundamental element of image editing software.

Rectangle tool

The standard tool for selecting an area of an image is a rectangle or, in some cases, an ellipse. To select an area, choose the relevant tool and then drag it from the top left corner of the selection to the bottom right corner.

Freehand drawing tools are renowned for being notoriously jerky and difficult to use accurately. Allow yourself plenty of practise before you embark on your 'live' project.

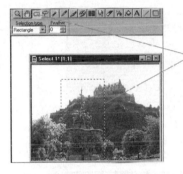

The Rectangle tool can be used to select part of the image. This can then be edited independently of the rest of the image

Freehand tool

The freehand drawing tool goes by a variety of names (Lasso, Trace or Freehand) but it does the same job: it selects irregular objects such as people, animals or plants. To do this, select the tool and then trace around the area that you want to select. Don't worry if you include too much in your selection; this can be edited using feathering or cloning.

If you are making a selection with the Freehand tool, make sure that your mouse is working properly. If it is worn or sticks then selecting a freehand area will be a frustrating process.

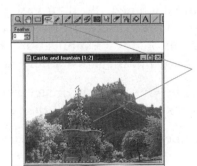

The Freehand tool can be used to draw an irregular outline around an object

Once an area has been selected there are various options available:

- It can be edited independently of the rest of the image. This is particularly useful if you want to apply an editing technique (such as blurring) to one part of the image

Copying and pasting is very effective for creating symmetrical patterns, where one item is repeated several times.

- It can be Copied and then Pasted back into the same image. This gives a duplicate image that can be effective if you want to create an effect such as instant twins

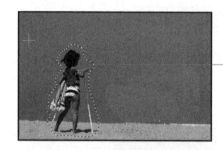

1 Select an image and then Copy it

If you are pasting a subject from one image to another, make sure that the background of the subject merges with the background of the new image. This can be done through the use of cloning — see Page 124.

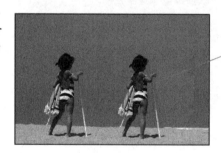

2 Paste the image to create a duplicate. Take care when you are positioning the duplicate image

- It can be Copied and then Pasted into a different image. This is useful if you want to import a particular image into another application or if you want the image to appear against a new background

- It can be Cut from the image altogether. This can then involves cloning to fill in the resulting space

- It can be dragged to another part of the same image

Cropping an image

Cropping is a technique that is frequently deployed in the reproduction of photographs in newspapers and magazines. It involves removing an area of the picture that is considered distracting or unnecessary. Now, with the wonders of digital editing software, this invaluable service is available to all digital photographers.

Some editing programs suggest an automatic cropping option when you want to crop something. While this can be useful in some instances, you do not have to use this option and it is usually best to select your own area for cropping.

Different editing packages handle cropping in differing ways but the general procedure is:

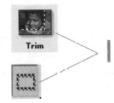

1 Select the Trim option, or a specific selection tool

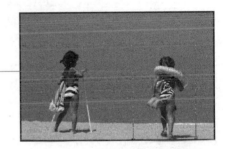

2 Outline the area of the image that you want to keep

In some packages, if you crop an image and then decide you want some of the background restored you can do this by expanding the image with the cropping tool — the cropped part has not been deleted, just hidden.

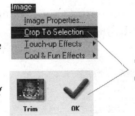

3 Select Crop... or OK

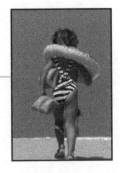

4 The unwanted part of the image is then removed, leaving only the selected part

Reducing red-eye

Even the most basic editing programs offer a wide range of effects and touch-up techniques that can be applied to your images. In some cases this is done by dragging the relevant icon over the image and then applying the chosen technique. In more advanced programs, filters are used to select the relevant options. This is done by selecting the area that you want the technique to affect, then choosing the relevant filter. Some programs have up to 80 different filter options but it is unlikely that you would need this many.

Some digital cameras come with a reduce red-eye option. This usually works with varying degrees of success and it is not something that could be called an exact science.

Reducing red-eye

Anybody who has ever used a camera knows about red-eye, the condition where a perfect portrait is ruined because the subject comes out with menacing red eyes as a result of the flash reflecting in the pupils when the picture was taken. This still happens with digital cameras, but at least the software is now able to remedy it and give your subjects back their normal appearance.

The methods of reducing red-eye vary between programs but the fundamentals are similar:

Red-eye can also be removed by cloning the affected area (see page 124).

1. Zoom in on the eyes

2. Select the affected area

3. Using one of the paint tools fill the red area with the desired eye colour

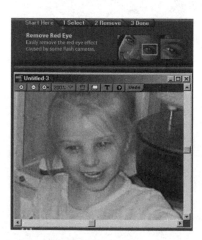

Most image editing programs have an auto reduce red-eye function

Sharpening

At first sight, sharpening appears to be the answer to every photographer's prayers: a tool that can improve and sharpen the focus of a blurred image. While sharpening can be a great asset to the digital snapper, it should not be seen as an excuse to try and take anything but perfectly focused pictures in the first place. However, sometimes blurred images do occur and sharpening is one way to try and improve them.

Most software sharpening tools have the minimum options of Sharpen, Sharpen More and Sharpen Edges, although the first one will usually give the most realistic effect. The more sophisticated programs allow for manual sharpening by specific amounts.

The technical side of sharpening involves the editing software adding extra definition along the borders between the dark and light areas of an image, or the areas with the highest contrast. This makes those borders stand out more. Once this effect is applied to the entire image it gives it the appearance of being in sharper focus.

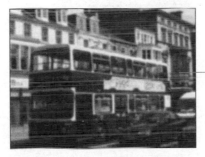

| A blurry image is unsatisfactory

2 Select one of the Sharpen options from the Filter menu

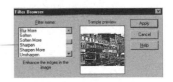

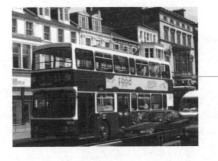

3 The image is still not perfect but at least it is more recognisable

Blurring and softening

Blurring and softening are essentially different degrees of the same effect. They can be used for two main purposes:

- Emphasising a particular object in a picture by softening the background

- Creating the impression of speed by blurring the background behind a vehicle:

Softening is a more subtle effect than blurring and is best used for backgrounds in portraits.

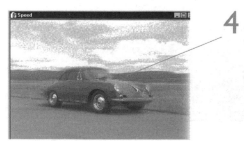

I Select the image with the Freehand tool and then Copy the selected image

When selecting the amount to blur an image, do not get carried away or else the background will lose all definition.

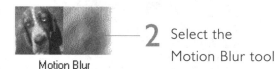

Motion Blur

2 Select the Motion Blur tool

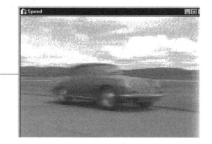

3 Apply motion blur to the whole image

4 Paste the copied object back into the image and position it in exactly the same place. If necessary, apply feathering to the edges (see over)

Feathering

This is a useful technique when you want to merge two images together. It is particularly effective when, as above, one of the images is in sharp focus and the other is blurred. Feathering ensures that the join between the two is seamless.

Feathering is usually used when a part of the image has been cut or copied so that the rest can be edited (typically when you want to create a blurred background). The cut or copied area can then be pasted back into the image. At this point feathering can be applied so that the hard edges of the non-blurred image merge into the blurred background.

When you are applying values for blurring and feathering within the same image, use the same amounts for both techniques. This way the blurred and feathered sections will match exactly.

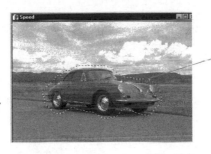

Select the image with the Freehand tool

Feather

2 Select the Feathering tool

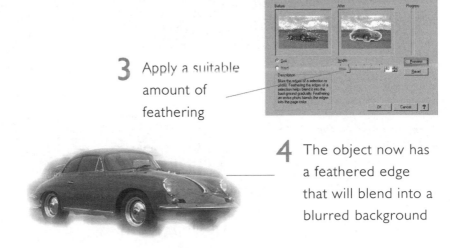

3 Apply a suitable amount of feathering

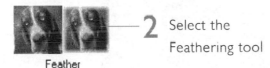

4 The object now has a feathered edge that will blend into a blurred background

Cloning

One of the main items on a digital photographer's 'wish list' is the ability to remove unwanted items and then fill-in the resulting space with the same background as the rest of the picture. What was once thought of as the realms of science fiction is now perfectly possible with editing software and is known as cloning.

The cloning tool works by duplicating pixels next to the selected area. You select the pixels you want to use as your cloning pixels by clicking on them with the cloning tool. Then, with the mouse held down, you move the cloning tool over the area that you want to change. The effect is similar to painting over a picture with a different colour.

One of the main uses for cloning is for removing blemishes and unwanted marks. This is the type of technique that magazines use frequently to make their models look as perfect as possible (which gives a modicum of reassurance to the rest of us). In this instance a mole or wrinkle is covered up by cloning the area of clear skin next to it.

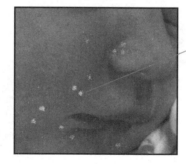

If an image has minor blemishes (such as spots), these can be removed by cloning the area next to them

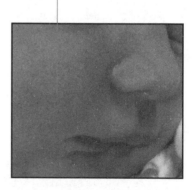

Cloning tools can be selected in a variety of sizes (thin to thick) and at times it is a bit like an artist trying to fill in a gap in a painting.

Cloning can also be used to remove larger objects from an image such as people or buildings. This is a more complicated procedure and could involve cloning from several parts of the image if it covers various colours and shades of background.

When you are removing objects with cloning, make sure that you also remove any shadow that they create in the image. Otherwise, you may end up with a case of a shadow being cast by an invisible object.

1 Open an image. This is an excellent image for removing the girl on the right because the background behind her is clear and uncluttered

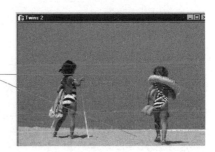

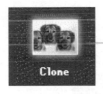

2 Select the cloning tool

3 Select an area that you want to use as the cloning area

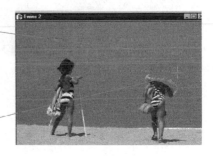

4 Move the cloning tool over the object to be removed

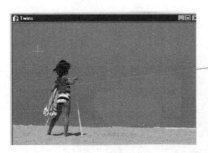

5 Once the cloning is completed the rest of the image can be edited using copying or cropping

Recognising jaggies and noise

Jaggies and noise are two technical terms that have emerged from the digital imaging industry (every industry has to have its own jargon, it seems).

Jaggies refers to the loss of definition in an image that has been compressed or enlarged too much, resulting in a jagged rather than a smooth image. This gives the image a grainy appearance that can have its uses for artistic effects but it is not very desirable if you want to have a smooth image. Jaggies are more likely to affect images with fewer pixels.

Noise can be caused by a lack of light on the subject when the picture was taken and gives a grainy result. Noise can be edited using image editing software, but the end result is not always perfect.

Both jaggies and noise can be edited by applying a slight blur or softening to the image. However, this can result in the main subject being out of focus. This can be improved by selecting the subject and then applying Sharpening to it.

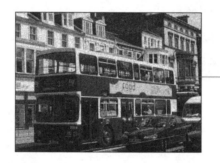

1 Noise causes a grainy, speckly image

2 To improve the image, select a Despeckle or Remove Noise filter

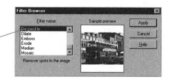

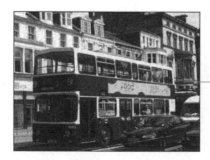

3 The image now has a much smoother appearance

Further editing options

There is a wealth of options available within digital image editing programs. This chapter takes a look at some of them including: using layers, adding text and colour, repairing damaged photographs and creating panoramic views.

Covers

Chapter Eight

Using layers

Layers, which are supported by some image editing programs (most notably the Adobe ones) but not all of them, is a function that allows the user to create multi-layered images that are built up with different image elements and items such as text.

Layers are a very useful way to add elements to an image without altering the original image — new elements are placed on top of the base image. An individual layer can be edited without affecting any other layers in the image.

The text layer is always present, even if you do not add any text. In this instance the layer is not visible. Also, it is not possible to delete or move the text layer.

Layers are controlled by the Layers Palette:

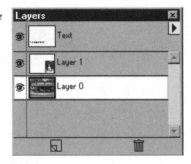

Some programs do not have a layers option. If you think you will be using this a lot then look at one of the Adobe products or Paint Shop Pro.

An original image starts off with only a single layer. However, if text is added to the image this is automatically added as another layer. Once the text has been placed on the image it appears on the Layers Palette. This can then be edited at any time, if desired, by selecting that layer from the Palette.

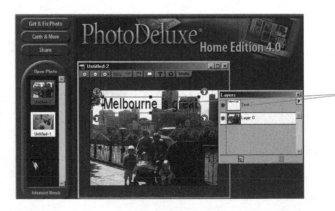

Text can be added and edited by using the Text Layer

Up to 99 layers can be used in one image and these can be included:

- By dragging another image onto the active image

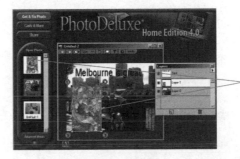

To create a new layer, drag an open image onto the one you are working with

- By dragging a layer from another image

- By pasting an image that has been copied

- By using the Layers Palette

When a layer is added to an image it goes on top of the ones that are already there. However, it is possible to edit individual layers by selecting them in the Layers Palette. This does not change the order of the layers. It is also possible to merge layers, but this should only be done once the entire editing process has been finished.

Layers are an excellent way to create complex images and can result in interesting effects:

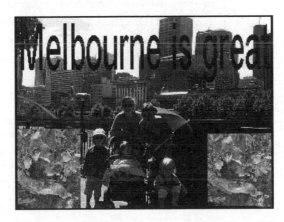

Creating collages

Collaging is a technique that involves taking elements from two or more images and combining them into a new composition. This can be done to create a humorous effect by setting two incongruous items together or as a photomontage to accompany an article in a newspaper or magazine.

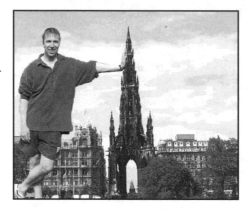

Collages can be fun, informative or outrageous

Although collages can be very effective, the following should be remembered:

- Use collages sparingly. If they are used frequently then their impact will be lessened and the effects will be wasted

- Plan you images beforehand (if possible) if you are going to be creating collages. For instance, if you want a collage of someone leaning against the top of a tall building, take one shot of the building and another of the individual leaning with their arm outstretched. This will make the editing a lot easier

- Make it obvious that the collage is not an original single image. Do not use them to mislead people

- Do not use collages to put people in embarrassing or compromising positions. This is particularly relevant if you are going to create a collage at work or place it in a publication that will be widely read

Once you have the images that you want to include in a collage you can create it with the following technique:

1 Open the images that you want to use to create the collage:

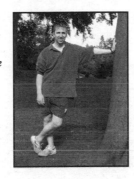 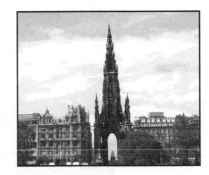

2 Use the Freehand tool to select the first object. Delete the background

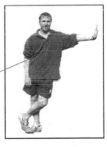

3 Copy the selected object and paste it into the second image

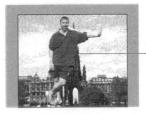

4 Resize the objects and make any minor adjustments using the cloning or colouring tools

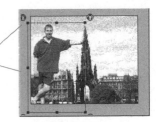

Panoramas

Any photographer who has ever stood in front of a majestic panorama of scenery is likely to have several photographs that have been taken in series to try and capture the full sweep of the view. Newer APS (Advanced Photo System) cameras have a setting that does this in one image, but digital photography goes one better by combining several pictures into one image:

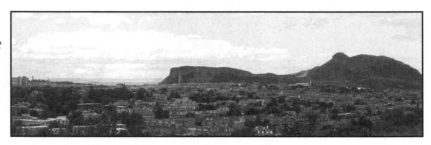

Some standard image editing packages have the capability for creating panoramas (known as stitching) and there are also dedicated software packages for this purpose, such as Spin Panorama (Web site at www.pictureworks.com) or PhotoVista (Web site at www.livepicture.com).

When creating a panorama there are a few rules that should be followed:

- If possible, use a tripod to ensure that your camera stays at the same level for all of the shots

- Make sure that there is a reasonable overlap between images. Some cameras enable you to align the correct overlap between the images

- Keep the same distance between yourself and the object you are capturing. Otherwise the end result will look out of perspective

- Keep an eye out for unwanted objects that appear in the panorama — if you are not careful they may appear in each frame

Stitching functions in much the same way as manually creating panoramas: select your images, put them in order and then stitch them together. Practise may be required to get exactly the desired effect but the basic technique is:

If you do not have a tripod for panoramic shots then try steadying your arm against something like a tree or a rock.

1 Capture the images that you want to make into a panorama:

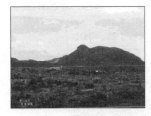

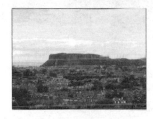

Take at least two images for each part of a panoramic shot. This allows a bit more versatility when matching images together.

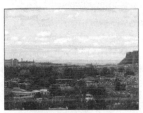

2 Select the images from within the stitching software

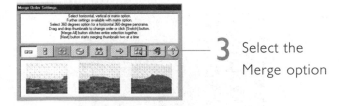

3 Select the Merge option

4 The images are now merged into one and can then be saved in the same way as any other image

Adding text

Adding text to digital images is a straightforward and effective way to personalise them and add individual messages. When you add text you begin by selecting the Text tool as you would in any word processing or desktop publishing program. However, the main difference is that the text is then typed in a dialog box and only inserted into the image once you have pressed OK. Once it is on the image it can then be moved around and edited.

Do not add too much text to an image. It can make it appear cluttered and draw attention away from the image itself.

Adding text to an image:

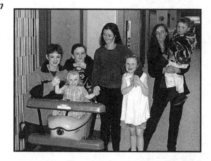

| Open an image

If you are adding text on a dark background then make it a light colour; if it is on a light background then make it dark. Some colours, such as yellow, do not always show up very well as text.

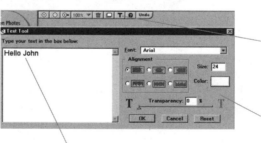

2 Select the Text tool: **T**

4 Apply formatting to the text

3 Enter your text

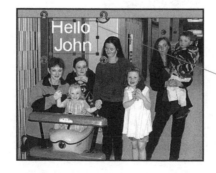

5 The text appears on the image in a text box and can then be moved around or edited

Adding colours

Additional colours can be painted onto an image in much the same way as adding text. This can be useful if you want to change a background element, such as the colour of the sky, or alter the colour of a piece of clothing.

To add additional colour to an image (from PhotoDeluxe):

Use small brush sizes for adding precise details to colours and a larger one to cover big areas.

1 Open an image

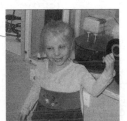

2 Select the Brush option

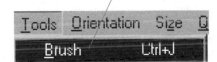

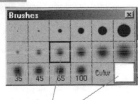

3 Select the colour and brush width

When you are adding new colours to an image, try and make sure that they blend in well with the ones that are already in the image.

4 Colour the object by moving the Brush tool over the selected area

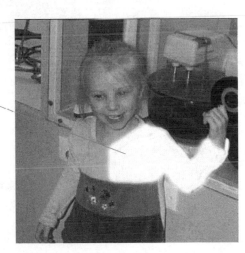

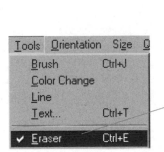

5 If necessary, the Eraser tool can be used to rub out the colour that has been added

Special projects

The use of printed images does not have to be confined to standard prints on A4 paper. There are several other options that enable you to create a range of original and striking items or gifts.

When you are selecting an image to transfer onto a T-shirt, make sure that there is a reasonable border around the main subject. This is because the software may trim the image if it is too big to fit properly onto the transfer.

Transferring images to T-shirts

Having a unique image on a T-shirt is a good way to stand out from the crowd and is surprisingly easy:

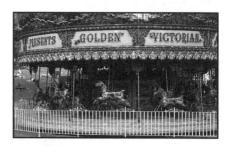

1 Open the image that you want on a T-shirt

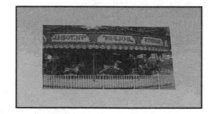

2 Print the image, in Mirror Image mode, on T-shirt transfer paper. The image will appear in reverse

Make sure you have the transfer sheet the right way up when you iron it onto the T-shirt. Otherwise you will ruin your transfer, and possibly your iron too.

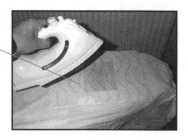

3 Iron the image onto a T-shirt

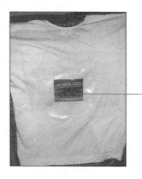

4 The image is now on the T-shirt

Cards, labels and calendars

Most entry-level editing programs offer a good range of cards, labels and calendars that can be used for presents or family gatherings.

The technique for creating these items is similar in most programs:

 You can print cards on either normal or photographic quality paper. However, if you use glossy photographic paper then the card will have a more professional appearance and it will be sturdier since this type of paper is thicker.

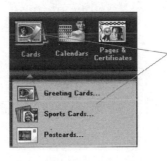

1 Select Cards and the type of card you want to create

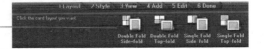

2 Select a layout

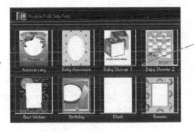

3 Select a background template, such as Congratulations or Birthday Wishes

 Some programs are rather slow at processing data for cards and they take up a lot of memory in doing so. If possible, make sure that you do not have too many applications open while you are creating cards.

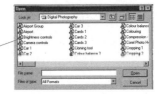

4 Select an image to fit on the card

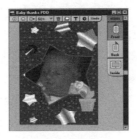

5 View the final version and edit if necessary

Effects and distortion

Also known as Filters and Browsers in some professional level programs, special effects and distortions act like magic mirrors on images. Depending on the chosen effect, they can change the appearance of an image and bend it into weird and wonderful shapes.

The basic editing function of effects and distortion is straightforward: you open an image and then you select a menu that will look like one of these:

Try not to overdo the amount of distortion that you apply to images. This may produce what is a striking image to you, but someone who is not so familiar with it may not be at all sure what the image is.

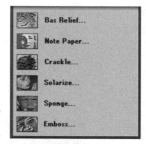

This dialog box from PhotoDeluxe offers various texture options

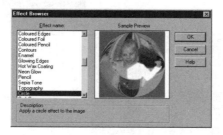

This one from Paint Shop Pro 7 gives options for changing the image's appearance

Other effects have dialog boxes into which values can be added to adjust the level. This is useful as it offers a greater degree of sophistication when applying the effect.

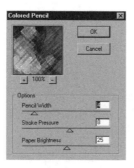

This effect in PhotoDeluxe gives the impression of a picture created with coloured pencils. The boxes allow the user to set values for the overall format

Uses for special effects

Although it can be great fun to add distortion effects to images of friends and family and colleagues at work, there may come a point when you want to do something a bit more constructive with the special effects in your editing software.

Most image editing programs have dozens of special effect filters. Experiment with them all, but you will probably end up with about half a dozen favourites that you use most often.

With a little planning and organisation it is possible to apply special effects that create an imaginative and eye-catching image, rather than just a humorous one. The key to success is to experiment with the special effects first and then think of images to capture that will best complement these effects.

Some suggested uses are:

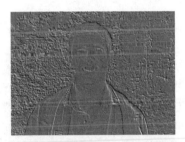

Use embossing to create metallic looking 3-D images. These can be particularly effective on Web pages

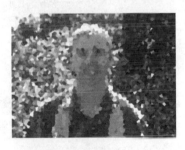

Use an impressionist effect for your own works of art

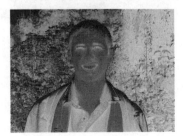

Use a negative effect to create an image for a photographic topic

Creating a slideshow

A slideshow of your favourite images is an excellent way to display them and can bring a new twist to a birthday party, or even a multimedia business presentation.

Windows Me also has a function for creating slideshows. See page 92 for details.

Some image editing programs have basic slideshow options but by far the most effective is the one supplied with PhotoDeluxe. It is called PhotoParade and it allows you to insert your images into an animated presentation of your choosing. You can then run this on your computer as many times as you like. The effect is dramatic and it makes the creator of the slideshow look very slick too.

Creating a PhotoParade:

1 Select PhotoParade>Create a PhotoParade from the Cards and More toolbar

When you are creating a slideshow be careful not to put too many images in it. You want the audience to be dazzled by the effect of the show, not put to sleep by its length.

2 Select the Album tab and the Open Album button and make sure that the PhotoParade button is selected in the My Photos window

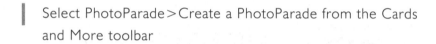

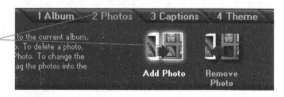

Try to maintain a consistent style and appearance when you are capturing images for a slideshow. This will give the final presentation a slicker and more uniform appearance.

3 Select the Photos tab and the Add Photo button. Select the images that you want to include

4 Select the Captions tab and the Add Caption button

PhotoParade is a software package bundled with PhotoDeluxe. More information about it, and additional add-ons, can be found on the Web site at www.photoparade.com

5 Enter a name and, if required, a comment for each image in your PhotoParade

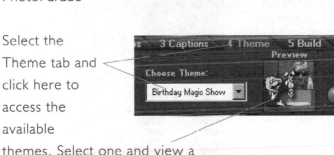

When adding captions and comments, each image has to be selected in turn and then the Add Caption button selected.

6 Select the Theme tab and click here to access the available themes. Select one and view a thumbnail preview here

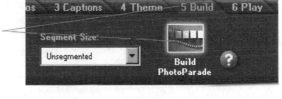

Other image editing software, such as MGI Photosuite, also has slideshow capabilities and these can be run with various elements such as background sound.

7 Select the Build tab and the Build PhotoParade button to create your show

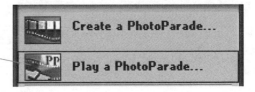

8 Select the Play tab and the Play a PhotoParade button to view the finished slideshow

Repairing old photographs

Image editing software is an excellent option for restoring the quality of old photographs or ones that have been torn or crumpled. In order to do this you have to get them in a digital format for the editing process. This can be done by:

- Scanning the photograph. This is the best option and if you do not have a scanner yourself then it could be done by a colour-copy print shop. Try and get the original image scanned as large as possible as this will make it easier to work with

- Capturing an image of it with a digital camera. This works best if you have a macro close-up facility

If you want to restore an old photograph it can be made to look even more realistic by adding a sepia tint to the image. If the editing package has this facility it is usually found in the touch-up toolbox or menu.

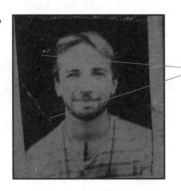

Image editing software can make dramatic improvements to images that are faded, torn or scratched. This is particularly useful for old black and white photographs

Before you start removing tears and lines from the image there are a number of steps that you can take to improve the final image:

- Adjusting the colour and contrast. If the colour quality of the image is not very good to begin with then it will not improve once you have given it a smoother look. Test different colour settings to see which ones look the best

- Applying a neutral background. This can be particularly effective if the picture is a portrait that has been taken against a plain background. If this is full of blemishes then it would be a lengthy task to correct all of them. A better idea is to select the subject, copy it, then paste it into another file

Once you have a digital image of the old or damaged photograph it can then be edited using the following procedure:

If you want to repair a damaged print properly, it is essential that you take your time. In all probability you will have to clone numerous different areas to cover all of the blemishes and this is a task that will have to be performed dozens of times in order to cover all of the different colours of the image.

It will probably also be necessary to work with the Cloning tool set to a small size so that you can zoom in and work in close-up detail.

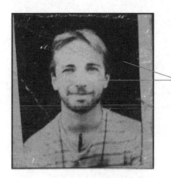

1 Adjust the colour and contrast

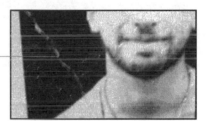

2 Zoom in on the affected area.

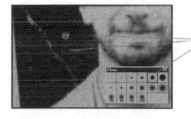

3 Select the Cloning tool and the area to be cloned. Repeat this with all of the affected area

4 Once all areas of the image have been repaired, adjust the colour and contrast again

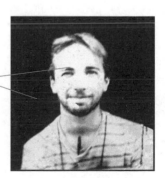

Creating patterns

Digital images are ideal for turning into patterns. This can be done to create a surreal effect or as a specific design feature:

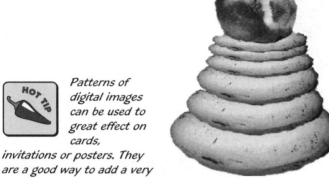

Creating a pattern effect:

1. Select the image that you want to use, using the Freehand tool

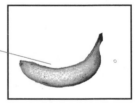

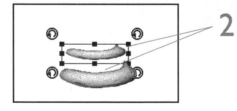

2. Resize and reshape as desired and then Copy and Paste to create the pattern

3. Add any new elements and size them as required

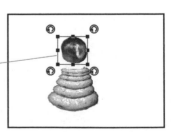

Creating a digital library

Creating image directories and the cataloguing and indexing of images are all important parts of the digital process. This chapter looks at how to save and maintain your images so that you can always find what you want.

Covers

Chapter Nine

The value of a digital library

When you have captured and edited your first digital images the natural reaction is to excitedly print them off, put them on a Web page or email them to friends and family. While this is perfectly understandable, it is sensible to limit this to a few images at first, just to get the novelty of the whole process out of your system. Once you have done this it is good practice to start thinking about creating a catalogued library of your images on the computer.

Since some digital cameras can hold over 100 images at any one time it is essential that they are all named and indexed when they are downloaded. Otherwise you will end up with hundreds of images such as DC176 and DC419, which is not much good for identification several weeks later.

Keeping the numbers in check

Initially, it may seem unnecessary to create a library of all of your images. After all, you will remember what they all are by their unique file names, won't you? Not necessarily. In two or three years time when you have hundreds, or even thousands, of images on your computer you may forget what 'Family cat' refers to. However, if it has been catalogued properly then you should be able to conduct a search and find it.

Indexing systems

The basic theory behind an indexing system is that each image is placed into a database and then assigned certain key words, such as 'holiday', 'France', 'wine' and 'Simon'. When it comes to looking for the image, these words can be entered as the search criteria. Anyone who is familiar with using a standard database will feel at home with an image cataloguing tool.

Creating a digital catalogue is not the most exciting part of digital photography but it is one of considerable importance, particularly in the long term.

The benefits

Most of the benefits of creating a robust catalogue of your digital images are fairly self-evident:

- You will not feel overwhelmed by hundreds of unordered images

- You will be able to search for your images under a number of different criteria, in case you forget the main heading under which they were indexed

- You will be able to search for every image that is catalogued under a certain criteria

Creating image directories

Creating new directories

The first step in cataloguing your images is to create separate directories, or folders, on your computer in which to put them. As your portfolio grows, so too will the number of directories, so create a new directory for each category of your digital images. To create a new directory or sub-directory (in Windows):

Keep your directories in a logical format i.e. family, work and hobbies.

Once you have the main directories for each topic, sub-directories can then be added for specific items.

On a Mac, new directories can be created using the Finder and the File>New Folder command.

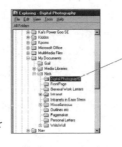

In Windows Explorer, select the directory from which the new one will appear

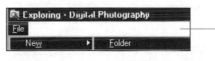

2 Select File>New> Folder

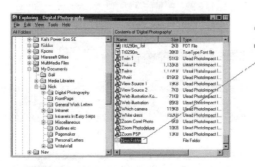

3 The new folder appears under the directory from which it was created. Give it a name

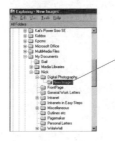

4 The newly named folder will now appear as a sub-directory of the main directory. Numerous sub-directories can be added this way

Cataloguing programs

Programs that allow you to download, save and store images come in two main varieties:

- Software utility programs

- Dedicated image cataloguing programs

Software utility programs

These are programs which allow you to download images from your camera, or another digital device, and then move them around on your computer. They also offer very basic image editing choices. They are excellent programs for viewing your images and placing them in specific directories on your computer. However, they do not offer indexing options. Two of the best types of these programs are Kodak's Picture Easy and EasyPhoto.

Digital cameras and scanners usually come with some form of cataloguing software — in some cases a basic utility and in others a more sophisticated indexing tool.

More information about Picture Easy and EasyPhoto can be found on the Web sites at www.kodak.com and www.easyphoto.com respectively.

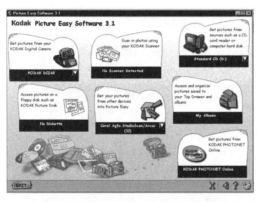

Kodak's Picture Easy has a user-friendly interface for downloading images...

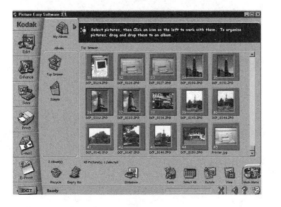

...and also for viewing them

Indexing programs

Programs that are designed specifically for indexing images work slightly differently from general cataloguing utility programs. They create databases that *relate* to the images involved but the images themselves are untouched — it is a database of information about the images, rather than the images themselves.

One such indexing program is ImageAXS, which, like Picture Easy or EasyPhoto, presents the pictures as a collection of thumbnail images. However, the toolbars associated with this program allow for a variety of indexing and searching options, as we will see later in this chapter.

In ImageAXS, the thumbnails are records of the images (rather than the images themselves), and the toolbars offer powerful cataloguing choices.

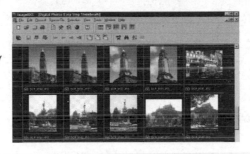

An indexing program like ImageAXS looks similar to a utility cataloguing one but there are differences – see the tip

Viewing image information

Both utility cataloguing programs and dedicated indexing ones enable the user to easily view file data about specific images. This is usually done by right-clicking the mouse on the relevant image.

Note that ImageAXS comes in the following versions:

- *ImageAXS 100*
- *ImageAXS*
- *ImageAXS Pro*

For more information, take a look at the Web site at www.dascorp.com.

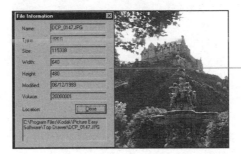

Important file information is easy to obtain in both utility and more sophisticated cataloguing programs

Saving and naming files

When a digital camera captures an image it gives it a numerical value, usually from 1–999. Once it reaches 999 it goes back to 1. So, unless you rename your files when you download to your computer, you will end up with a lot of meaningless file names.

If you are downloading your images with a program such as Kodak's Picture Easy, the images will appear as thumbnails on the screen, with their numerical name underneath:

If you are using a serial cable connection to download and save your images it can take a long time. If one is available, use a USB connection.

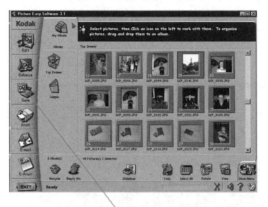

Images are downloaded from a camera with simple numerical values e.g.: DCP_0103.JPG

If you are using dates in your file names e.g. for birthdays or anniversaries, do not use the following format: 1/9/2001. This will not be accepted as a valid filename. Try 1~9~2001 instead.

Files can be selected and Saved onto your computer's hard drive. This can either be done individually or as a batch

Windows Me offers an effective interface where you can view images in Windows Explorer and rename them too. For more information on this see page 90.

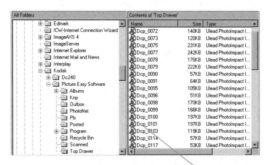

If files are Saved directly into a directory on the computer then they have the same numerical value

Save and rename

An alternative to saving an image with a numerical file name straight into a directory is to select a Save As function and then give it a new name when selecting a directory for it. In Picture Easy this is done by double-clicking on an image and then:

When you are saving images of people, use surnames in the file name, not just first names. If you have a lot of images of different people called John then it could get a bit confusing.

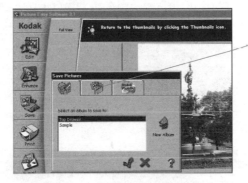

1 Select the 'Save files elsewhere on your computer' icon

It is generally quicker to save files to a directory first and then rename them.

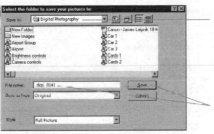

2 Select the directory where you want to put the file

3 Give the file a new name and then select Save

Renaming saved files

Another way of changing file names is to do so once they are in a directory. This can be a useful option if you have downloaded a lot of files in a single operation. To rename a file this way:

- Open Windows Explorer

- Select the file

- Select File>Rename, type the new name then press Enter

Creating an index collection

If you want to create a collection for some, or all, of your images then an excellent indexing program is Adobe ActiveShare. This is free and can be used to download, name and index images and it also has functions for sharing them over the Internet.

In addition to its image sharing capabilities, ActiveShare also offers some image editing functions, although they are not as extensive as the ones in dedicated image editing software.

ActiveShare software

ActiveShare is provided with PhotoDeluxe and it can also be downloaded from the following site:

*   www.activeshare.com/

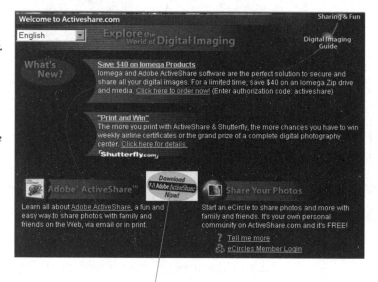

Click here on the ActiveShare Home Page to download the ActiveShare software. You will be taken step-by-step through the process and ActiveShare will then be downloaded onto your hard drive

Creating albums

The ActiveShare interface offers options for sharing images over the Web and it also allows you to store and edit your images. This is done by creating a reference to where the images are located, rather than downloading the images themselves. The first step in this process is to create an album where you are going to keep images in ActiveShare:

 ActiveShare is an excellent option for creating image albums so that you can view a lot of images quickly.

1 Select Create Album

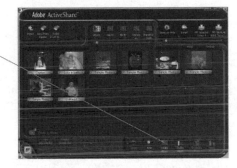

 Numerous albums can be created but only one can be opened at any one time. Double-click on an album to open it.

2 In the Create Album dialog box, select a name for the album and where you want to store it — on your computer or on a type of removable storage. Select OK

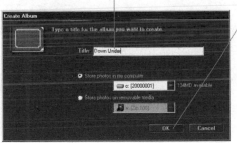

 For more on sharing digital images on the Internet, see Chapter Eleven.

3 The new album appears here

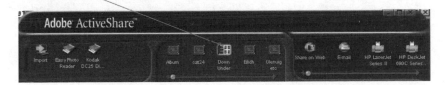

Importing images

Images can be opened in ActiveShare from either the hard drive, a digital camera or a scanner:

1 Double-click on an album to open it

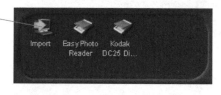

It is possible to load more than one image from the hard drive at a time. Hold down Ctrl when you are selecting the images and then click on all of the ones that you want to copy into the open ActiveShare album.

2 Select Import to open an image from the computer's hard drive

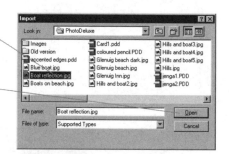

3 Select an image from the Import dialog box and select Open

4 To open an image from a digital camera or a scanner, click here to view the available options

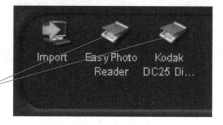

5 Select the appropriate device and then double-click on the device to access the images

Naming and finding images

Images in ActiveShare can be individually named and it is also possible to conduct a search through your albums to find specific images.

Naming images

Keep image titles short, so you can see the whole of them in the caption box.

1 When an image is opened in ActiveShare it is titled Caption

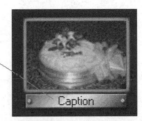

Words that are used in a search for images are known as keywords. These can match up with the same word or words in an image caption and they can also make a match if any of the keywords appear in the details of the source folder from where the image was imported. For instance, if an image came from a folder called Summer Holidays, a search using the keyword Holidays would find this image.

2 Click once on the image to select it and then click once on Caption to add your own name for the image

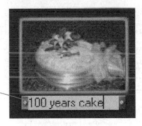

Finding images

1 Select Find Photos

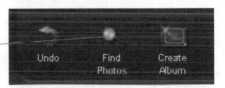

2 In the Find Photos dialog box, enter the search criteria and specify whether you want to search in a specific album or all of your albums. Select Find

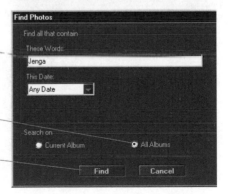

Cataloguing good practice

Cataloguing and indexing are a chore rather than a joy. However, when you have 10,000 images to search through you will be glad that you took the trouble to do this particular piece of image housekeeping.

When you first start creating catalogues and indices it is a good idea to follow a few self-imposed guidelines so that you achieve efficiency and consistency with your indexing. Here are a few to consider:

- Do your cataloguing and indexing as soon as you have downloaded your images. You may not feel like it at the time, but you certainly will not feel like it days or weeks later

Programs for indexing and cataloguing images are like the shoe-boxes of the film world. It is easy to stuff things into them and forget about them. Try and avoid this and keep your files up-to-date.

- Create new directories and folders for each area of your image collection

- Give your images meaningful names, that will be clear to you in several years' time

- Use a dedicated indexing program and take the time to become familiar with it. This will pay off in the long run

- Always try and be consistent with keywords and data for fields. Always put the same type of data in the same data field for each record

- Back-up your index files in the same way as you would with any other files

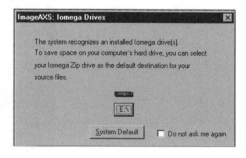

ImageAXS offers a start-up option of saving your files to a Zip drive, if there is one fitted. This is worth considering for back-up purposes

Getting a hard copy

The printing process is an integral one in digital photography. This chapter looks at some of the options available and how to obtain the best printed images possible.

Covers

Chapter Ten

The printing process

Colour printing is one area of modern technology that has advanced as much as any in recent years. What was once the domain of professional printers, or a select few who could afford expensive colour printers, is now available to anyone with a spare £100 or more to spend.

It is not essential to know exactly how each type of printer works to produce the end result but it is useful to know a bit about the methods they employ. The two main forms of colour printing are:

When you are dealing with halftone printers the term 'separations' may come up from time to time. This refers to the individual colour screens that the process creates. These are usually combined to create the overall image but they can also be printed out individually.

If you are working with a commercial printer they will probably ask to see colour separations of your images.

- Halftone printing

- Continuous tone printing

Halftone printing

Also known as screens, this is the method used by inkjet and laser printers. The image is created by printing a series of dots, or screens, that create the illusion of being a continuous image. However, if you look closely at a halftone image you will be able to see the individual dots of colour. As the technology improves it gets harder and harder to identify the dots and when the image is looked at from a normal viewing distance the halftone patterns should not be visible to the naked eye. One problem that can occur with halftone printers is that, if the different screens are not lined up properly, then the final image will suffer from shadowing and the colours will not look entirely accurate.

Halftone printers usually work on the CMYK (Cyan, Magenta, Yellow, Black) colour model while continuous tone printers generally employ the RGB (Red, Green, Blue) model.

Continuous tone printing

This is the method that produces the closest output to true photographic quality. Unlike halftone printing, there is no separation between the colour elements of the image and so each part of the image merges seamlessly into the next. If you examine a continuous tone image carefully you will not be able to see the coloured dots in the same way as you can with a halftone image.

Continuous tone printing is used for printers such as dye-sublimation and it is the route to take for the best images.

Printer resolution

As with digital cameras, the resolution of an inkjet printer is one of its main selling features. Resolution for printers of this type is measured in dots per inch (dpi) and, as a rule, the higher the better. Some inkjets currently on the market can print up to 1440 dpi. However, it should be remembered that the printer resolution does not affect the size of the image; this is done by the image resolution setting in the editing software. To recap:

- One measure of image resolution is the number of pixels per linear inch and this can be set within the image editing software. So if an image is 1200 pixels wide and you want a printed image that is 4 inches wide then the image resolution should be set at 300 ppi (pixels per inch)

- Printer resolution is not the same as image resolution but most printers work on a minimum output basis of 300 dpi. If a printer prints at a higher resolution it just recreates each pixel using more coloured dots of ink. This increases the quality but does not affect the overall size of the image

Image resolution can be selected within image editing software and this is what determines the final printed size:

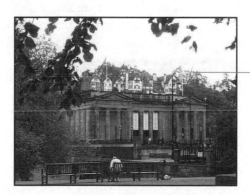

At different resolution settings within editing software, an image will be printed at different sizes

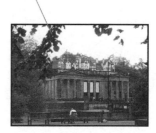

Printer settings

One area that is often overlooked when outputting colour images is the printer settings that can be adjusted via your printer software. All printers come with software that enables them to communicate with a computer and vice versa. In the computer world these are known as *drivers*, which makes it sound more like a piece of hardware, but it is in fact software.

If you are unsure about what options are available via your printer software, consult the manual. This may open up a variety of new options on the printing front.

Adjusting settings

Printer settings can be adjusted when you select Print >Setup from whichever program you are working in.

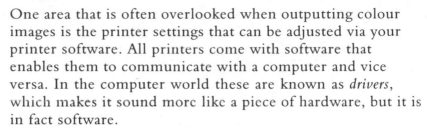

A standard print setup box. This enables the user to select the manner in which the image will be printed and also the final output quality

If you print your images by selecting the print icon that appears on most toolbars then the printer will use the current print settings. If you want to change anything you will have to do it via your Print dialog boxes or a program such as Print Manager.

Take some time to experiment with different printer settings for your images. They do make a difference and it will increase your confidence in the overall editing process.

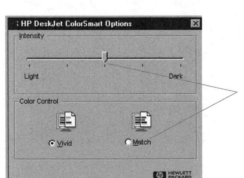

This dialog box allows for adjustments to be made to the intensity of the colours and to match output colours with the colours on the monitor

Printing speed

Headline figures

For once in the computing world, speed is a bit of a red herring as far as colour printing is concerned. Most inkjet manufacturers claim their products can print between 2 and 8 pages per minute in colour. This can be a major selling point but there are two things to say about this:

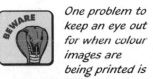

One problem to keep an eye out for when colour images are being printed is paper warp. This occurs when the weight of the ink on the paper causes it to warp and buckle. Try and test for this before you buy a printer.

- This figure is usually for the printer when it is set to its lowest quality setting i.e. draft or economy. This is suitable if you want to get a preview of what your image will look like but it should never be used for the final product

- The headline pages per minute figure is for when you are printing images on standard multi-copy paper. Inkjet printers react differently when they are set to print on different paper types — the better the paper then the slower the print speed

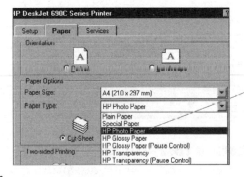

Colour inkjets offer a selection of options for paper types. The higher the quality of paper, the longer the image will take to print

The larger the image, the longer it will take to print. If you want a full A4 size output then this will take a lot longer than for a standard 6 x 4 photo-size print.

Realistic figures

If you want to get the highest quality of print, on the best paper, the output figure is more likely to be in terms of minutes per page rather than pages per minute. However, for most people who are printing images this does not really matter. Quality certainly beats speed in this case, and so be prepared to wait if you want sharp images. If you also need a printer to produce textual documents then the print speed may become more of an issue.

Inkjet printers

If you want to use digital images for anything more than displaying on a Web page or a monitor then a good quality colour printer is essential. Without it, the images from the highest resolution camera could look grainy or slightly blurry.

Three of the top inkjet printer manufacturers are Epson, Canon and Hewlett Packard. Their Web sites can be found at (respectively):

www.epson.com/

www.canon.com/

www.hp.com/

The most common type of affordable colour printer on the market is generically known as the inkjet printer. This was a name that was first coined by Hewlett Packard to describe a particular printing process and it has since spawned numerous imitators. Two other companies, Canon and Epson, use a similar method but they apply different names; bubblejet for Canon and micro piezo for Epson. Although the technology between the three differs slightly, they are all usually grouped together under the term inkjet.

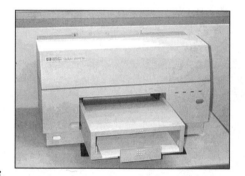

Colour inkjet printers are now a common sight in both the home and office

If you want the best results, then printing images on inkjet printers is not cheap, in terms of running costs — around 30 pence per page is average. Always ask for these costs when you are buying a printer.

What's it for?

What you intend using your printer for may determine the type that you buy. Some colour inkjets are designed specifically to produce high quality colour images. They can also print text, but the quality is not as good as a printer designed specifically for that purpose. They also tend to be less economical when printing text. Other printers go for a combination of good colour images and text...

Decide what you are going to be printing and then investigate the market with this in mind. For the truly dedicated it may be a case of one printer for colour images and one for text. The low prices of these machines mean that this is feasible, but there is always the matter of space.

The inkjet method

Inkjet printing is essentially a simple process: tiny dots of coloured ink are placed onto paper by a collection of miniature nozzles. This is usually done with two cartridges, one containing black and the other containing cyan, magenta and yellow. When they are combined they create the CMYK (K is for black) colour model.

Some colour printers only have a single cartridge and this usually results in inferior colour quality. This is because they cannot produce the same range of colour and their version of black is not true black, more like a murky brown. Always go for printers that have two colour cartridges.

A handful of more recent inkjet printers have an additional two colours (lighter shades of magenta and cyan) as well as the four in the CMYK model. This increases the colour variations available and is effective for subtle colour changes such as skin tones.

Always allow colour prints to dry thoroughly before you handle them. Depending on the size of the print, and the type of paper, this could vary from a few seconds to a couple of minutes.

Black and colour inkjet cartridges cost approximately £15–£30 depending on the printer type. However, refill packs can be bought for about half this price. This involves refilling the cartridges yourself but it is worth it for the cost savings.

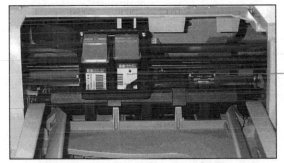

Go for inkjet printers with 2 print cartridges, black and colour

Although inkjet technology has advanced in leaps and bounds in recent years it still does not match traditional photographs in terms of quality. However, the printer companies are pouring significant resources into developing this lucrative market and the end result is improving all of the time. In terms of combining colour and monochrome output these types of printers are hard to beat, particularly at their low retail prices.

Other types of printers

Dye-sublimation

An increasingly popular type of printer for colour images is the dye-sublimation variety. Also known as dye-sub or thermal-dye printers, this is one option that is worth considering if you are only interested in printing high quality colour prints. Dye-sub is a process that heats various coloured dyes in such a way that they are fused onto the paper. Unlike the halftone effect of inkjet printers, dye-sub printers create a continuous tone image in which the individual dots of colour cannot be seen. This gives an excellent end result and is probably the closest you will currently get to traditional photographic standard.

Consumer-level dye-sub printers begin at around £200. However, the price-per-page is higher than an inkjet printer and you do not always have the option of printing in draft quality.

One recent feature of dye-sub printers is the ability of some of them to be able to generate prints directly from a digital camera, as well as printing from a computer. The camera is connected to the printer and a hard copy can then be produced. While this is a useful feature, it removes the editing element so you have to make sure that your pictures are exactly right when they are captured.

One downside of dye-sub printers is that the consumer-level models are sometimes restricted in their output size and they do not handle large volumes very well. Also, dye-sub printers can only be used for printing images. So if, like most of us, you want to print text on occasions, you will need another printer to do this.

Some dye-sub printers only take one format of memory card, i.e., either SmartMedia or CompactFlash. If you are considering a printer of this type, make sure it accepts the type of memory card that you use in your camera.

Thermal wax and micro dry

Thermal wax printers use a similar heat method to dye-sub but are cheaper for running costs. Micro dry printers also use heat to affix colour to the page but in this case it is done through ribbons coated with special inks. This gives a good quality at a reasonable price.

Although dye-sub, thermal wax and micro dry printers are not as ubiquitous as inkjets, their profile is likely to rise as consumer interest in digital photography really begins to take off. So expect to hear more about these types of printers in the future, particularly when they are able to produce plain text in addition to colour.

Laser

As a rule, laser printers are faster than inkjet ones and provide a better print quality. However, their main drawback is cost, particularly for colour printing. Monochrome laser printers are reasonably priced but colour ones are usually prohibitively costly for the home user. Unless you are willing to spend a lot of money to have your images printed at a higher quality, then colour laser printers are best left for the office or professional print bureaus.

Not only are laser printers expensive, so too are the toner cartridges, particularly if you buy the brand name ones. There are reconditioned cartridges available and these can usually be obtained from companies who advertise in computer magazines.

One way around this is to have your images printed by a high street commercial outlet. This is done by taking a disc of your work to the print shop and then asking them to output your images on a laser printer. This will be cheaper than buying a laser printer, but still relatively expensive. Weigh up the cost against the final quality you are looking for. It is a useful option to consider for special occasions or a one-off production.

Pros and Cons

When you are looking at printer options it is worth considering the following points:

- Do you want a printer just for photographic images, or for images and text?

- Can you afford two printers, one dedicated to images and one for text?

- Do you want to print images larger than A4 format?

- Are you aware of the print costs per page of the printers you are looking at?

- Are you aware of the cost of the consumables (paper, ink etc.) for various printers?

- Will you be using the printer for high volume printing? This may be the case if you are using it in a business environment, so bear this in mind

Selecting paper

Paper types

While one piece of paper may look similar to another, the differences can be considerable when it comes to printing photographic images. Some inkjet printers can give good results on plain A4 paper, but if you switch to a type of paper specifically designed for colour images then you will notice the difference immediately.

If you want the best print results then go for the best products: a high resolution printer, photographic quality paper and a photographic ink cartridge.

Some of the various paper types available include:

*   Standard multi-copy paper. This can be used in inkjet printers, laser printers, fax machines and photocopiers. It is very versatile but gives the poorest quality for photographic images

*   Inkjet paper. This is a step up from multi-copy paper and gives good colour results on inkjet printers. It is useful for printing items such as company reports that have coloured charts and similar images

The reason that glossy photographic paper can produce results which are so much better than ordinary multi-copy paper has to do with the coating on the surface of the paper. It is designed to grip the ink more securely so that there is less chance of dots blurring into each other.

*   Photographic quality paper. This is a generic term for glossy paper that produces results which are as close to photographic quality as you are going to get from an inkjet or laser printer. It is the most expensive type of paper and within this range there is a considerable selection from the main companies such as Epson, Kodak, Hewlett Packard, Agfa, Canon and Ilford

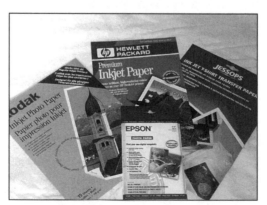

Experiment with different types of paper to see which is the best for the job you are doing

Other printing options

Although the most common paper format is A4 this is by no means the only option available. Depending on the type of printer, the following mediums and formats can be used:

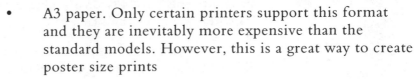

If you are printing images for an OHP presentation, make sure that they are sharp and clear once they are projected onto a screen. In some cases, colour definition and image detail may be lost.

- A3 paper. Only certain printers support this format and they are inevitably more expensive than the standard models. However, this is a great way to create poster size prints

- Film transparencies. These are sheets of clear plastic that can have images printed on them for display on an Overhead Projector (OHP). This can be very useful for business presentations and if you have some of your own images it will make a pleasant change from the ubiquitous Clip Art

- Cards. Images can be printed on special size cards. This can also be done onto A4 paper and then cut to size, but if you want a professional finish then this is a useful option

- T-shirt transfers. A relatively new product on the market. The image is printed onto the transfer, which is then ironed onto a T-shirt

Branded or generic

Some printers, such as the Epson Stylus 3000, can print up to A2 size. However, a printer such as this will cost in the region of £1300.

Each printer manufacturer has their own brand of photographic paper and they all insist it is the one that works best with their own unique printing system. But in reality there are a lot of other companies that produce photographic quality paper that is of an equally good quality.

One of the main considerations when buying paper may be the cost. The top quality paper is not cheap and you can sometimes save money if you buy paper from companies other than the printer manufacturers. Shop around and test different paper types. It may take a little time until you find a good combination of price and quality.

Ink issues

Photographic cartridges

Some inkjet printers come with optional photographic ink cartridges. These should only be used when you want the very best quality and you are using photographic quality paper. If you have a two cartridge printer, the photo cartridge replaces the black one.

When you change cartridges in your printer, make sure you realign the print cartridges. This is done via the printer options and is particularly important for photo cartridges — if the alignment is even slightly out then this will affect the colour of your printed image.

Photo cartridges can improve the quality of images but on the downside they are more expensive than normal ink cartridges. In general, photo cartridges cost in the region of £20–£30 upwards. Each manufacturer declares that you should only buy their own brand but in reality there are a lot of cheaper imitations that do an acceptable job.

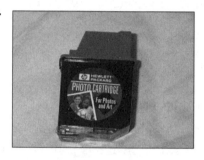

Colour photographic cartridges give the very best quality when printing colour photographs

Dealing with fading

It is a fact of digital life that images printed on inkjet printers will fade over a period of time. If an image is kept away from direct sunlight then it can survive for two or three years before it starts to fade. However, in direct sunlight the fading process may begin after a few months.

Photo cartridges usually come with a dedicated storage container. Keep the cartridge in here whenever it is not in use. It will protect the ink nozzles and prevent the ink from drying out.

One way to lengthen the life-span of your images is to spray them with water-fast sprays that are available in art supply shops. This gives the image a certain amount of general protection and some sprays also give a degree of protection against sunlight.

Because of this tendency for ink to fade, it is essential that you always keep copies of your favourite images on your computer or backup device. This way you can always print another if the original fades beyond recognition.

Using a print bureau

As digital photography gains in popularity the printing world has not been slow to embrace the possibilities that this presents in the way of printing colour images for customers. They offer a variety of services and the two main advantages of getting your images produced professionally are:

- Quality. Print bureaus have access to the type of printing equipment that would not be found on the desk of the average home user. This ensures the best quality for your images

- Size. Unlike consumer printers, professional bureaus can print in a variety of sizes: from standard A4 size up to A1 size in some cases

Using a high-street outlet

Some high-street developing outlets are beginning to offer services for creating prints from digital images. However, at the moment, the majority do not offer this service so it is a matter of phoning around to see who does what.

A better bet in this respect is contacting a colour copy shop. These are outlets that specialise in items such as colour photocopies and colour printing. They are more likely to be abreast of the latest digital technology developments and they should be able to produce prints from either a CompactFlash or SmartMedia memory card. Again, check the Yellow Pages for details in your area.

Professional bureaus

These are high-quality professional printers and it is not the type of place to go if you just want a couple of snapshots developed. Cost is a major issue here and you will probably only use their services if you are contemplating a major print job such as a book or high-quality promotional material. Before they start your printing job, a professional bureau will want a lot of specific information: file format, colour separations, colour matching and so on. If you use this type of service it is essential you talk to them first about your needs.

Printing checklist

Since the printing process is, in some cases, the final one that will be applied to your images before they go on view to the world, it is worth following a checklist for achieving the best possible prints:

Check your printer's manual to see what advice it gives for print settings for optimum output of digital images.

- Choose an inkjet printer for a good combination of quality, price and versatility. These are the most commonly available printers and it is possible to find them sold in packages with many computers these days

- Choose a dye-sublimation printer for the very best print quality. These are excellent for printing photographs but they cannot print text and some of them are restricted as to the format in which they can print

- The size of your final image will be determined by your image resolution. This is set by the image editing software. Use 300 dpi as a standard for printed output

- The resolution of the printer improves the quality of the printed image but it does not affect the size

The colour printing process and the technology behind it are improving on an almost daily basis. Check the computer magazines to see what the latest innovations are and which new products are on the market.

- Use normal paper and a draft quality setting on your printer for preview prints of your work

- Use photographic quality paper, photo ink cartridges and the highest quality print setting on your printer for your final prints

- Try not to get fingerprints on photographic quality paper before it is used. This may affect the printed image

- Leave prints to dry for up to five minutes to ensure they do not smudge or smear

- Use a protective coating on your images before you display them. This will increase their longevity

Images on the Web

Digital images are ideal for including on Web pages or for emailing around the world. This chapter shows how to include them on the Web and the best ways to present them on this constantly expanding medium.

Covers

Chapter Eleven

Why use the Web?

Two good books that provide a general look at the Internet and Web page creation are:

- *'The Internet in easy steps'*
- *'Web Page Design in easy steps'*

both in the Computer Step range.

Like it or not, the Internet and the World Wide Web are slowly but surely invading all aspects of our lives. What was originally the domain of computer geeks and programming fanatics is becoming increasingly mainstream and accepted in modern society. The uses that it can currently be put to are growing constantly:

- Contacting people around the world in an instant with the use of email

- Checking world news via international newspapers

- Conducting banking transactions

- Trading in stocks and shares

- Buying goods and services, from groceries to antiques

This is just the tip of the Internet iceberg and its uses are expanding almost on a daily basis. So does it matter if people have no interest in the Internet and what it does? Quite possibly, yes. An increasing number of businesses already have their own Web sites, and email and Web addresses are becoming more common in both the personal and the business world. The Internet revolution is here to stay and those who ignore it are in danger of being swept away by a tide of technology. Most people would find life a lot harder if they did not have a telephone and the Internet looks sure to command this level of importance in our lives in years to come.

There is a lot of jargon and hot air spouted about the Internet by people who like to think it is a medium specifically for the computer-minded. This is not true and it is a good idea to steer clear of these people. The best way to learn about the Internet is to get online and start surfing.

As the Internet becomes more widely accepted and used, so more people will want to register their own presence on the Web. This is where digital images come in: it is increasingly rare for Web sites *not* to include some images and if this is the first stop for either personal or business information then most people will want to include their own images on the site. Through the use of a digital camera or a scanner anyone can create professional images that they will be proud to have displayed all around the world on the Web.

Preparing images for the Web

When you are capturing images for use on a Web page there are a few factors that have to be taken into consideration: it is not just a question of snapping away and then slapping it onto a Web page:

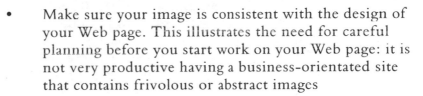

Back in the dark ages of the Internet, some browsers had difficulty displaying images. This problem is long gone now and images are considered a normal part of Web life.

The only time problems could arise is if you want to incorporate your images into advanced Web functions such as banner adverts. Some browsers will support these and some will not.

- Capture your image at your camera's or scanner's lowest resolution and highest compression. As discussed in the next section, file size is of paramount importance for images on Web pages. The general rule is, the smaller the better. Since computer monitors should be able to display even the lowest resolution image (640 pixels x 480 pixels) at a size of approximately 9 inches by 5 inches this should be big enough for most uses

- Make sure your image is consistent with the design of your Web page. This illustrates the need for careful planning before you start work on your Web page: it is not very productive having a business-orientated site that contains frivolous or abstract images

- Emphasise the subject of the image. If necessary, crop out an unwanted part of the image and increase the size of the main subject

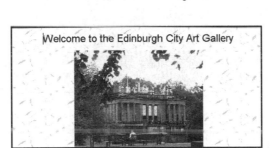

This image is perfectly acceptable for a Web page...

However, it is improved by cropping and enlarging the main subject

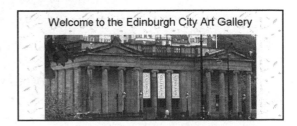

File size, file size, file size

If there is one thing that should be remembered above all else for images that are to be displayed on the Web, it is file size. The bigger the file, the longer it takes to download through a modem and onto a browser. And the longer it takes, the more frustrated the user becomes. It has been calculated that Web users are prepared to wait for no longer than 17 seconds for a Web page to download. After that they become increasingly irritated or move on to another site altogether, possibly never to return.

When you are considering the issue of images and file size the following points should be near the top of your checklist:

- Do you really need to include the image? Does it add anything to the Web site or are you including it because you like the image yourself?

- Can the image be made smaller? For instance, could it be cropped so that any superfluous parts of the image are removed?

- Can the image be included as a thumbnail? This enables the user to see a small version of the image, which they can click on and enlarge if they are interested

Another consideration for file size and downloading time is that not all users will have the most modern modems with which to access your pages. The current fastest modems operate at 56 Kb per second, while some older models only transfer data at 33 Kb or 28 Kb/sec. If you feel this is going to be an issue for your pages then be very frugal with your images. If you are not too concerned then design your pages with the fastest modems in mind and hope that those who need to will upgrade at some point.

If you are using images on a personal Web page then downloading time may not be such an issue. But if you are creating a corporate Web site or an intranet then there should be a clear policy regulating the use of images.

Web authoring options

Although most image editing programs have an option for publishing images on the Web this is more of an image preparation tool rather than a Web page authoring tool. If you are serious about producing Web pages then you will have to either take a crash course in Hypertext Markup Language (HTML) or use a dedicated Web authoring program such as Macromedia's Dreamweaver or Adobe's Go Live. The reason that an image editing program is not sufficient is simple: a Web site is, or should be, more than just a collection of images. You will almost certainly want to include text and, before long, you may want to get involved with items such as tables, frames and forms.

An excellent starting point for learning about HTML is 'HTML 4 in easy steps' in the Computer Step range.

If you want to create a Web page there are four ways to go about it:

- With raw HTML in a text editor such as Notepad. For this you will need to have a reasonably good knowledge of HTML coding

- With an HTML editor such as HotMetalPro. Again, HTML knowledge is required, but programs such as this make it a lot easier to create HTML files

For a detailed look at Dreamweaver, have a look at 'Dreamweaver in easy steps' in the Computer Step range.

- With a dedicated Web authoring program. There are various ones on the market and three of the best are Macromedia Dreamweaver, Microsoft FrontPage, Adobe Go Live

- With the 'Convert to HTML' function that programs such as Microsoft Word and Microsoft Publisher have

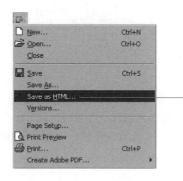

More and more software programs have a Save As HTML option, which converts a document into a Web-ready format

What is HTML?

This is not the time or the place to get into an in-depth discussion of HTML, but suffice to say it is a coding format that tells a Web browser how a particular page is to be viewed on screen. It does this by placing opening and closing 'tags' around each element on the page. So if you want to have a piece of text displayed in the largest headline size, you would place the <H1> </H1> tags around it.

If you are new to it, HTML can seem very complicated at times. But it is not a full-blown computer language and the basics can be picked up reasonably quickly. In some ways it is similar to the type of word processors that were around during the 1980s — the basic text was typed on screen and then formatting tags were added for items that were required to be in bold, italics, underlined or the suchlike.

If you want to see what an HTML file looks like then open any Web page, select View>Source and a window with the source HTML will appear.

BEWARE

Some HTML coding includes items such as Java and JavaScript. These are mini programs and they are a lot more complicated than basic HTML. If you come across this when you are viewing source files do not worry about it. This is one area that is best left to the experts.

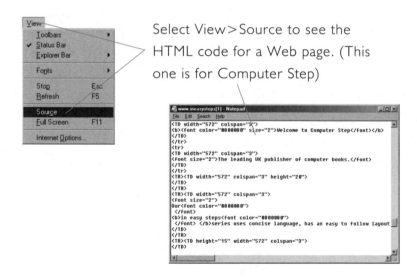

Select View>Source to see the HTML code for a Web page. (This one is for Computer Step)

Do not be put off by your first sight of HTML. Even if you are not a computer genius you would be able to produce a modest HTML Web page in a matter of minutes, with a bit of assistance.

For the record, the HTML coding for inserting an image into a Web page is as follows:

<img src="myimage.gif">

Additional HTML tags can then be added to determine the size and position of the image.

It is perfectly possible to create effective and striking Web pages without even knowing of the existence of HTML. This is done with what is known as a WYSIWYG (What You See Is What You Get) program. This is a type of program that removes the need to create the source HTML code yourself — what you layout on screen will be, more of less, what the user will see on their browser. Your page design is automatically converted into HTML behind the scenes by the program.

Anyone who is familiar with desktop publishing programs will feel at home with a WYSIWYG Web page authoring package because the two processes have considerable similarities.

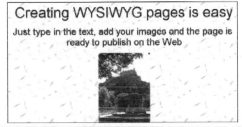

Creating WYSIWYG pages is easy

Just type in the text, add your images and the page is ready to publish on the Web

When you place an element on a page in a WYSIWYG program, it is automatically converted into HTML, ready for Web publishing

HTML can be learnt reasonably quickly and it is a good investment, as it could save you a considerable amount of time in your Web authoring career.

Despite the power and ease-of-use of WYSIWYG programs, it is nevertheless a good idea to learn the basics of HTML before you start your career as a Web page designer. The reason for this is that it is sometimes easier to make subtle changes to a page by altering the source HTML code rather than changing the elements on the laid-out page. Also, WYSIWYG programs have a tendency to take over the page creation process and create what they think you want rather than what you actually want. If this happens it can be more effective to do the editing in the source HTML.

Knowing the basics of HTML is a bit like learning about how a car engine works: you do not have to know it to drive the car, but it could come in handy if it breaks down.

WYSIWYG editors

FrontPage

If you are creating commercial Web sites or you are going to be doing a lot of Web page creation at home then a serious contender as a Web authoring tool has to be Microsoft FrontPage. This is a powerful WYSIWYG program that offers a lot in the way of additional elements, such as rotating banners, hover buttons and page themes.

FrontPage has two elements: a page editing element (FrontPage Editor) and a Web site management element (FrontPage Explorer). You create your pages in Editor mode and then review your overall site structure in Explorer mode.

Creating Web pages in FrontPage is simply a case of typing and formatting your text and then adding additional elements through the options on the menu bars.

One particularly useful FrontPage function as far as images are concerned is the estimated downloading time that appears in a box at the bottom of the Editor screen. This gives an estimate of how long it will take to download that page on the Web. This enables you to add images, review the downloading time and then edit them accordingly. Even so you should always test your pages in a live situation and also bear in mind that users will be using different modems and browsers to download your pages.

Microsoft have a particular liking for the name Explorer for their software. Their browser is an Explorer, the latest file manager system is an Explorer and it also pops up in FrontPage.

Make sure you know which one is being referred to when you hear this ubiquitous name.

The estimate displays in the bottom right-hand corner of the FrontPage screen.

In this example, 62 seconds is too long so the page would have to be revised.

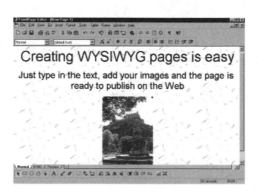

FrontPage gives you an estimate of how long pages will take to download

Dreamweaver

This is Macromedia's WYSIWYG tool and it is one that is preferred by professional Web designers and enthusiastic amateurs alike. It is an extremely powerful program that offers both a simple interface and tremendous flexibility for the user. It combines various palettes to assist the WYSIWYG authoring process with an effective HTML environment.

A 30 day trial version of Dreamweaver is available from the Macromedia

Web site at:

www.macromedia.com

The full package costs approximately £250.

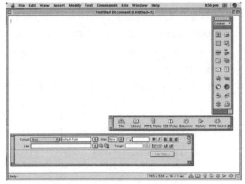

HotDog

This has a more complicated interface but it is packed full of features and is a very powerful tool once you get the hang of it. However, some knowledge of HTML is presumed as this is a combination of an HTML editor and a WYSIWYG Web authoring tool.

A 30 day trial version of HotDog is available from the Web site at:

www.sausage.com.au

The full package costs approximately £75.

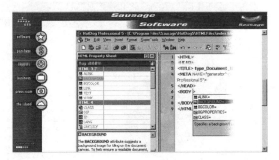

HotDog combines HTML editing with powerful WYSIWYG features

Including images on a Web page

Style

Even if it is true that a picture tells a thousand words, it is still sometimes necessary to offer a few words of explanation for an image. It is counter-productive to have a stunning image that seems to have no relevance to the rest of the Web page.

Before you start adding images to a Web page it is important to know how and why you are going to be using it, rather than just including them for no specific reason. There are a number of reasons for including images on a Web page:

- Information. If you are advertising a new product or telling people about a new addition to the family, your audience will want to see visual evidence of this

- Design. Images can be included on a Web site to compliment the overall style of the site. In some cases a visual theme can run through an entire site. If images are used in this way then they have to be of a certain standard so that they will gain people's attention

- Impact. Some images are so striking that they stop people in their tracks. This is useful for a Web site but it is important that a dramatic image is not offensive in any way. Also, images that create a strong impact should be changed regularly: the impact is diminished considerably if the image has been seen numerous times

Although the Web is not subject to any strict regulation, this does not mean you can get away with images that cause offence. You may not suffer at the hands of the law, but your Web site will very quickly wither if people are put off from visiting it.

This image is effective because it advertises a product and the design fits in with the rest of the page

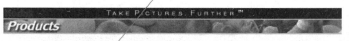

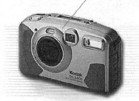

KODAK DC3400 Zoom Digital Camera

Make your pictures come alive with the KODAK DC3400. Get detail, brilliance, and user-friendliness you can expect only from the name you trust in pictures - Kodak.

- Get vibrant, detailed pictures for prints up to 8" x 10" with its 2MP resolution.
- Capture crisper close-ups with its 2X optical zoom. Get even closer with its 3X digital zoom.
- Shoot with ease - the DC3400 was built off the award-winning KODAK DC280 Zoom Digital Camera.
- Get connected easily with the USB and serial ports.
- Print pictures at home - it's as easy as 1-2-3. Use KODAK Inkjet Media with the KODAK Personal Picture Maker 200 by Lexmark to get brilliant color and long-lasting prints...

Size and orientation

Another consideration about how you are going to display your images online is their size and where they are going to appear on screen. The size of the image may be determined by where it is on the site: an image on the Home Page may require to be larger to catch and keep people's interest, while one further into the site could afford to be smaller. The key here is, once again, downloading time — it is no use having the most dynamic and innovative image if the user gets bored and moves on before it has time to download.

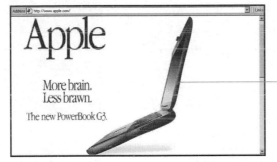

This Home Page image is simple and striking, emphasised by the white background

The same image appears (smaller) on a page within the site, thus maintaining consistency

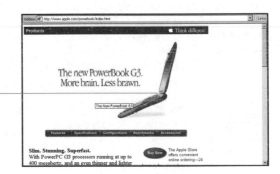

If images are being used as a specific design feature then it is beneficial to have them appearing at the same point on every page i.e. the top left-hand corner. This way the user becomes familiar with the page design and feels more comfortable navigating around the site. Creating a consistent style is an important aspect of any Web site.

Sharing on the Web

There are a number of Web sites that allow you to post your images and then invite specific people to be able to view them. This is like having a virtual photo-album that you can show to your family and friends on the Web. One of the most effective of these programs is Adobe eCircles, which is located at www.ecircles.com

eCircles can also be accessed from the Adobe Web site at:

www.adobe.com

Creating an eCircle

eCircles is free and you can become a member by selecting the Sign Up button on the Home Page and then following the on-screen instructions. You will be asked to provide a log in name and a password. Write these down and keep them in a safe place.

Major Internet portals such as Yahoo and MSN offer a similar service to eCircles, where you can download your images and then invite family and friends to come and view them.

1 Go to the eCircles Home Page, enter your login name (see Tip) and password and then select Log In

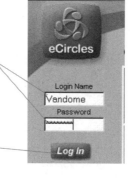

2 Select the Start a New eCircle button

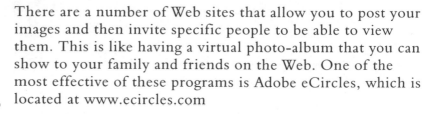

3 Under Private eCircles, select Share your photos

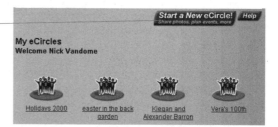

...cont'd

You have to add images to a new eCircle before you can invite people to view it.

4 To add images to your eCircle, select the Browse button and select images from your computer. Each image has to be selected separately and you can select up to 15 at a time

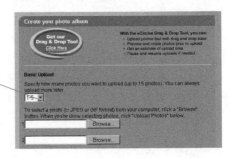

When inviting people to an eCircle, make sure you type their email

5 Once the images have been downloaded, select the Invite More People button.

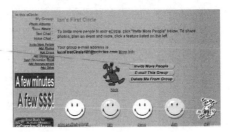

addresses correctly, otherwise they will not receive the invitation. If you are inviting more than one person, separate the addresses with a comma.

6 Enter the email addresses of the people you want to invite to your eCircle. Use the preset message that the recipients will receive, or write your own

Other people can invite you to view their eCircles too. If you want to remove yourself from a particular eCircle, open it and select the Delete Me From Group button.

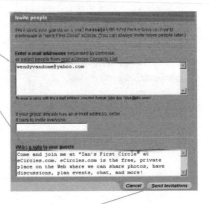

7 Select the Send Invitations button. A dialog box will appear telling you that the invitations have been sent successfully. Select Done

Emailing images

Email is one of the most accessible and effective elements of the Internet. Communication is fast and cheap and it is an excellent way to send images around the globe in seconds.

Some of the uses for email images are:

- Letting family and friends around the world know about a new arrival — and letting them see him or her

- Holiday snaps before you have even got home yourself

- Business use, such as emailing an image of a piece of equipment that has broken to see if an online solution can be found

- In crime prevention, emailing images of known criminals who may be moving around the country

Before you start emailing your images you should consider the format in which you are going to send them and the method the recipient is going to use to view them.

As with Web images, it is best to keep images for emailing as small as possible as this speeds up the downloading time. However, if the recipient intends to print out the image then you may want to increase the resolution so that they get as good a hard copy as possible. Weigh up these options of speed against quality, depending on the intended use.

Even if the recipient does not have an image editing program, they will still be able to view the image via their Web browser, as long as the file is in GIF or JPEG format. If they have an email connection then they will almost certainly also have a browser. To open an image all they have to do is double-click on the email attachment and the browser will automatically open it. It may be advisable to include instructions to this effect in case the recipient is unsure about what to do with the attachment.

...cont'd

The process of emailing an image is as follows:

Several images can be attached to an email. However, this creates a larger message to transmit and increases the chances of some of the data being lost on its journey through Cyberspace.

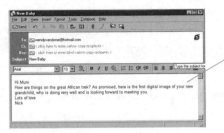

1 Open your email program and compose your email in the usual way

2 Select the Insert File icon, which looks like a paperclip (in Outlook Express)

3 Select an image

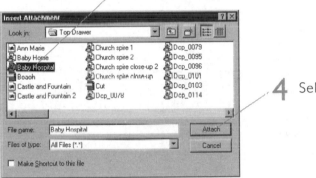

4 Select Attach

If the image that is attached to the email is not a GIF or a JPEG then the recipient will have to open it with an image editing program or a utility program such as Paint.

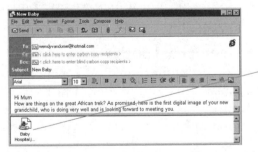

The file will now appear as an attachment at the bottom of the email. This can be opened and viewed by the recipient

Marketing images on the Web

If you have gone to the time and expense of setting yourself up as a digital photographer, it is only natural that you may want to try and benefit from your investment in the way of selling some of your images. This can be done by either setting up your own photo library and marketing it on the Web, or through an established agency or photo library.

Marketing your own image

If you want to sell your images via the Web then you will have to create your own site on which to advertise your wares. The design of this will depend on the market that you are hoping to attract but it should contain some standard elements:

- A general introduction about your site and the type of images on it

- Thumbnails of your images. These should link to the full size version, but make sure they are not of the highest resolution — you do not want people to download them and then be able to reproduce them. The best quality version can either be in the form of a higher resolution image on your computer or a colour transparency which could be posted

- A search facility so that users can search for images on particular topics

- Your terms and conditions for selling your images

- A copyright notice, stating how and where the images can, and cannot, be used

A commercial outlet

There are numerous photo agencies and syndication organisations on the Web. For most the quality of resolution required may be too high for the majority of digital photographers but two to try are:

- Mirror Syndication at www.mirpix.com

- PA News Photo at www.pa.press.net

Index

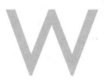